Leaping Over the Ocean

Leaping Over the Ocean

Re-Reading Black Women's Mobility
in the 19th and Early 20th Century
Trans-Atlantic World

Willi Coleman

Washington, DC

Copyright © 2020 by Willi Coleman
New Academia Publishing, 2021

All rights reserved. No part of this book may be reproduced or transmitted in any form or by any means, electronic or mechanical, including photocopying, recording, or by any information storage and retrieval system.

Printed in the United States of America

Library of Congress Control Number: 2021907831
ISBN 978-1-7359378-2-3 paperback (alk. paper)

New Academia Publishing, 4401-A Connecticut Ave. NW, #236,
Washington, DC 20008
info@newacademia.com - www.newacademia.com

For Maybell Robinson Carr
who wept into my bones
the assurance that no distance
was too far for me to travel
and
Tina Irving August Brown
who travels the world as if
she owns it.

Contents

Introduction	1
Chapter 1. Beginning: Sarah Mar'gru Kinson	7
Chapter 2. Sarah Parker Remond: From Salem, Massachusetts, to The British Isles. "Like Hot Lead to Pour on the Americans"	27
Chapter 3. Anna Julia Cooper: Answering The Call of "A Thumping From Within"	45
Chapter 4. Mary Church Terrell: Daughter of Privilege, Activist by Choice	65
Notes	95
Index	121

Introduction

Transatlantic travel was one of many social institutions benefiting from technological advances that became a part of life in mid-nineteenth century America. The movement of people and goods over the high seas increasingly became the work of steam-driven ships replacing vessels powered by sail. Travel abroad, or the "Grand Tour," once the prerogative of wealthy white males, slowly became desirable to and for their female counterparts. Either as appendages to men or on their own, white women increasingly appeared on passenger lists. As upper- and upper-middle-class women embraced ocean travel, ships became increasingly more comfortable for those in first class. With the vast majority of passengers being confined to steerage class, few luxuries would trickle down from those who were literally above them.[1]

Even as wealthy white Americans, both male and female, took to the high seas in order to pursue adventures on the other side of the ocean, an even smaller segment of the population was also boarding ships.

When viewed through a more finely tuned lens, the presence of African women and their descendants is irrevocably tied to the movement of peoples across the barriers of oceans. Hidden within the language of "travel," the coerced mobility of Africans during the transatlantic slave trade would position Black women as the single largest category of females traversing the Atlantic Ocean throughout the seventeenth, eighteenth and early nineteenth centuries.[2] They were at once invisible and occasionally noticed within the broader story of early ocean travel. As early as 1840, a particular representation of Black women aboard ocean-going vessels was crafted for public consumption. Attempting to amuse and perhaps educate land-bound readers, the American writer Thomas Haliburton shared his own vision of dark woman crossing the ocean. In an era when the overwhelming number of Black men, women and children in America were enslaved, Haliburton draws quite another picture. Black female passengers aboard his ship are free and mulatto, with questionable moral character. Unlike other passengers and Black crewmembers, these unmanageable women of unacceptable racial background provide the most scandalous reasons for their presence. Their time was spent attempting to attract the gaze of hapless white males and annoying other female passengers. The "real" ladies are of course white, and sorely put-upon by slightly tawny-skinned women whose looks and attire dare to rival their own.[3] It is assumed that their shipboard behavior was but a prelude to what was expected upon arrival in Europe.

By the early 1900s, a second and polar opposite version of Black female ocean voyagers had emerged. Still seeking public acceptance, this post-Reconstruction traveler was simply known as "Mammy." In *Mammy 'Mongst the Wild Natives of Europe*, novelist Ruthella Mory Bibbins unfurls the adventures of "old nurse mammy." Complete with numerous illustrations of a round, dark face atop a more-than-ample-sized body, the central character dominates more than 300 pages but is never given a name. She is "mammy," and the author leaves no question regarding either her race or the reasons for her "terrifying" voyage. Unlike her earlier mulatto sisters, the ex-slave-turned-servant now travels with her white "family" because she trusts no one else to care for "Miss. Jinny and the baby." Chock-full of malapropos and side-splitting social hiccups, this funny, loyal and aged Black woman finds life and white folks outside of her "home" in the United States unbearable. She is supplied with ample reasons to pray the "Lawd" will get her back home to America.[4]

Even as fictional Black "jezebels" board ships in search of white men, and aging ex-slaves find life outside of the United States not worth living, real Black women provided another image. Comparatively few in number, they boldly stepped aboard sailing vessels during the early stages of trans-ocean travel. Given the day-to-day circumstances faced by the overwhelming majority of Black people, such women represent a truly extraordinary slice of history.

The four women at the center of this work were born over periods spanning the approach of the Civil War through the cusp of emancipation. Remarkably, at least two of the four survived long enough to help launch the early stages of the modern civil rights era. None escaped the reality of slavery and its violent aftermath. Similarities in their choices and behavior were primarily governed by that fact, but it is the differences between them that can also serve to broaden our understanding of the many ways Black women of previous generations would negotiate and dare to expand the world they were forced to live in. Each of the women presented here serves to highlight different facets of slavery and freedom for Blacks and women. We begin with a small Black girl literally traveling from freedom toward enslavement before reversing her trip a second time. We move on to engage two more women whose life and earliest years were entrenched in America's "peculiar institution," but that fact alone does not ensure similarities in their experiences. Nor does their reality explain that of the fourth woman, who, though born free, thoroughly understood that geography alone allowed her to remain so.

Whatever their individual circumstances, all four women lived in a world demanding day-to-day submission in every facet of their lives. That each woman found her own specific reasons to travel beyond the land of her birth made them curiosities in their own time and among their own people, but their decisions to do so must reposition Black women within the discourse of early transatlantic travelers.

As such, we are given another thread that has to be unraveled in the broader understanding of human mobility during nineteenth and early-twentieth century globalization. Moving beyond hearth and home, race, gender and geography toward their own ends, these women were the living antitheses of the much-needed "mammy."

Mar'gru Sarah Kinson, Anna Julia Cooper, Sarah Parker Remond and Mary Church Terrell were all born within the long reach of slavery. One was born in Africa, one in a free state and two in slave states. Three of the four women crossed the Atlantic more than one time, and all experienced their first ocean voyage prior to the early 20th century.[5] Two of the four would find their final resting places outside of the United States. Out of this small quartet of women, one would eventually surface as the first African female to attend college in the United States. A second, born a slave in the American South, became the first African American woman to earn a Ph.D. from the Sorbonne in Paris. Crossing additional borderlines, she defended her dissertation in French, the topic daring to critique slavery in the French colony of Haiti.[6]

Recognition of the attainment of such stellar achievements is not the chief purpose of this work. It is instead the exploration of the lives of women who exercised their own agency while transgressing the triple boundary lines of race, gender and geography. In spite of the uncommon boldness of some of their choices, Kinson, Remond, Terrell and Cooper were neither the first nor the only Black women heeding the call of nineteenth century global travel. They represent only one strand within a larger framework. Long before emancipation, religion served to protect and propel Black women who successfully left the United States for other countries. Three of those who were made bold by their faith, Nancy Gardner Prince, Zilpha Elaw and Amanda Berry Smith, moved across the world neither as cargo, human merchandise nor servants. Spending decades outside of the country, each wrote memoirs or narratives documenting their extraordinary experiences. One of the earliest sojourners, Nancy Gardner, was a freeborn but impoverished native of Massachusetts. She recorded her decision to leave the United States with rather frank pragmatism: "Care after care oppressed me ... I found peace with God ... After seven years of anxiety and toil, I made up my mind to leave my country. September 1st, 1823, Mr. Prince arrived from Russia. February 15th, 1824, we were married...we embarked...bound for Russia." Her Mr. Prince, a man known to Nancy's mother, was a Black seaman who had been living and working in St. Petersburg. Returning with him to Russia, the new bride took in boarders and established herself as a seamstress. With her husband working as a servant for wealthy and titled Russians, the couple made their home for almost a decade. Following her husband's death, Nancy Prince made at least one trip alone to Jamaica, not returning to the United States permanently until after 1842."

Chapter One

Beginning: Sarah Mar'gru Kinson

In 1997, filmmaker Stephen Spielberg used his niche in popular culture to introduce contemporary movie aficionados to the idea of violent resistance aboard slave ships. Based on historical fact, his film *Amistad* told the story in true Hollywood style of that period. With white men at the center as both hero and villain, the script deviates to present a powerful central character that is African. Identified as the leader of a bloody rebellion was the undeniably Black Cinque. Captured in Sierra Leone, Cinque was appropriately dark-skinned and a notable specimen of masculinity. In both film and fact, his audacity captured the imagination. Among the hundreds of shipboard rebellions attempted, the name Cinque remains perhaps the best known.

Whether depicted in film as entertainment or presented through the works of erudite scholars, certain aspects of resistance aboard slave ships remain relatively obscure to this day.[1] Buried within the larger story is the fact that children witnessed, survived and may have participated in attempts to snatch freedom within the boundaries of sailing vessels. Without a doubt there were children aboard the infamous *La Amistad*, yet their stories remain relatively unknown. In fact, a normal feature of the transatlantic slave trade was the acceptance of children as an exploitable commodity in the business of human bondage. Research suggests that during the peak period (1825–55), vessels such as the *Jesus Maria* traveled with a "cargo" made up 98 percent of children. The very young were sold by Africans and purchased by European agents. Ship captains packed small bodies aboard vessels, physicians certified the state of their health, and the British legal system developed special codes for their transportation. Indeed, by 1788, the enslavement of Black children was both common and organized enough to encourage British Parliament to regulate the space allotted for them aboard ships. The legal language was refined in order to more accurately describe cargo that ranged in age from infancy through adulthood. Terms such as "woman-girl" and "man-boy" were used by some countries to designate those who were too young to fit into the category of young adult. Another identifier was that of height. Using that measurement, those shorter than four feet four inches were categorized as children.[2] In the name of efficiency it was also possible to simply count two children as one adult. Such decisions were based on several interlocking factors, including requests from potential buyers, the rules of companies responsible for insuring "human" cargo, and captains concerned with actual space aboard their vessels. No such pragmatic issues slowed the tide of children removed from the continent of Africa. In fact, one researcher found their numbers increased "from 22.7% in the eighteenth century to 46.1 between 1810 and 1867."[3] The lived reality of children aboard slave ships was shaped and controlled by such factors.

The saga of *La Amistad* began in Cuba in the summer of 1839. Under the flag of Spain, the ship sailed into Havana to take on board 53 Africans. While the institution of slavery was legal throughout the Spanish colonies, the transnational trade itself was a violation of both Spanish law and international trade agreements. Theoretically, after 1820, only Blacks who had been born in Cuba and their descendants could be bought and sold. This, however, did not curtail the bustling illegal trade in human cargo across the high seas. In Cuba and other marketplaces, the business of false documents, bureaucratic blindness, piratical ship captains and investor greed worked hand-in-hand with every aspect of the trade in Africans. Acceptance by the general populace was such that the enclosures in which slaves were held became tourist attractions. Laws and treaties notwithstanding, long before and after *La Amistad*, Cuba was enmeshed in a "well organized system of kidnapping."[4] Hence it is not remarkable that aboard *La Amistad*, a man named Jose Ruiz held ownership papers for 49 African males, while another, Pedro Montes, owned three girls and one boy. A second slave boy, Antonio, was the property of the ship's captain.[5]

The circumstances were so typical for what was expected to be a short trip from Havana to Puerto Príncipe that neither the owners nor their crew were prepared for what followed. Within a few days of setting sail, a full-fledged insurrection took place. After freeing themselves and killing the ship's captain and cook, the Africans threw the small crew overboard. With the apparent leader, Cinque, now in charge, Pedro Montes was ordered to return to the place from which the Blacks had been taken. While not in possession of the specific skills needed to navigate the vessel, the Africans knew that in order to sail home they must move toward the sun. With no intention of sailing to Africa, Montes deliberately wandered the ocean aimlessly hoping to cross paths with another ship.

Finally after two months, perilously low on food, several Africans dead from ingesting contaminated liquids, Montes piloted the tattered vessel toward the coast of North America. By August 25, 1839, the schooner reached the shoreline of Long Island, New York. Desperate for food and water, Cinque and two other captives made their way ashore. Before they were able to return with supplies they came into contact with a few amazed locals. It was then and there that the vessel and all aboard became an American story. The distressed ship was intercepted by the naval vessel *USS Washington* and towed to

New London, Connecticut. Once in port, local curiosity and rumors of Blacks hijacking a ship escalated to alarm. Newspapers from New York to New Orleans fed the public imagination with vivid images of dark-skinned, blood-drinking cannibals.[6] As expected, the suggestion of any form of organized Black violence against whites generated fear and civic outrage across the country. Once rescued, Spanish citizens Montes and Ruiz presented their versions of what had taken place aboard the ship. Ruiz, who could speak English, identified Cinque as the slave who led others in escaping their chains, killing crewmembers, and taking possession of the vessel. The story as presented automatically raised questions of international agreements, slave rebellion and piracy throughout the Western world. With Ruiz and Montes charging the Africans with murder and piracy, the supposed killers were taken to jail. Pending the arrival of a U.S. Circuit Court judge in Hartford Connecticut, the "men" were housed some 40 miles away in New Haven, Connecticut.

Not until the judge arrived was the presence of children unduly remarked upon. When commenting on the case, an observer recorded: "The three girls and Antonio, the cabin boy, are ordered to give bonds in the sum of $100.00 each to appear before the said court and give evidence in the aforesaid case, and for want of such bonds to be committed to the county jail in the city of New Haven."

Between the letter of the law and the business of slavery, four Black children and the "cabin boy" were ruled witnesses to, but not involved in, mutiny aboard a ship. Separated from the men, the youthful quartet was boarded in the jailer's home. The three girls were "much terrified at the separation from their companions."[7] Given the circumstances, there would be little reason to believe any in that pitiable and powerless group would, in time, make their own mark in history, yet at least one lived to do so.

One of youngest persons aboard *La Amistad* was Mar'gru, a girl whose name meant "Black Snake." Among the few Africans to survive the Middle Passage and see their homeland again, Mar'gru was one of an even smaller number of individuals to make a return trip to the United States as a free person. In addition, Mar'gru, who became known as Sarah Kinson, has the distinction of being the first African student to attend college in the United States.[8]

In the country that was America two decades before the Civil War, Mar'gru was just one small figure in an ever-growing state, national and international political and media spectacle. Along with more than three dozen adult men, she endured throngs of Connecticut citizens who clamored for a glimpse of the exotic Black foreigners. Some packed the courthouse while others willingly paid the jailer $12.50 in order to stare at the strangers. Some viewed the opportunity as entertainment; others found the captives' situation in conflict with their own strongly held religious and political beliefs.

As in other sections of the country, Connecticut had its own tortured involvement with slavery. While the earliest records of Black bondage in the state dated back to the Colonial era, laws moved toward ending the practice were found as early as 1774. Beginning with outlawing the importation of slaves by sea or land, Connecticut moved on to enact laws of gradual emancipation for those already in bondage. Additional legal statutes provided that children born of a slave mother would, after March 1, 1784, become free; however, such offspring were still required to "serve" their mother's owner until the age of 25. It would not be until 1848 that slavery was completely outlawed in Connecticut.

Hence, when *La Amistad* approached the shores of Connecticut in 1839, the institution of slavery was theoretically a dying tradition in that state. Although defined as legally free, most Blacks lived their daily lives within a form of truncated liberty. While they could and did file complaints and give evidence against whites in courts, they were not consistently allowed to exercise their right to attend local schools. Clearly, having Black skin in Connecticut did not translate to holding full human or citizenship rights.[9] During the decade of the 1830s, then, neither the statutes of individual states, the federal government nor international agreements could be said to represent the thoughts and feelings of "the" American people on the subject of slavery. Historian Richard Hofstadter described the period as "governed by ineffective leadership ... and above all cursed by an ancient and gloomy wrong (slavery) that many of its people have come to cherish as a right."[10]

The era had been ushered in by Nat Turner's slave insurrection in Virginia in 1831. Two years later, the admission of a Black female pupil to the Prudence Crandall School so outraged the citizens of Canterbury, Connecticut, that a mob promptly burned the building down. Crandall and her young charges barely escaped with their lives. Citizens not involved in mob violence also expressed their objections to Black education. The mere discussion of establishing a "college for the education of colored people" in New Haven led to so much consternation that one citizen wryly suggested moving it to Cornwall "because the ladies of that town readily give themselves ... to colored gentlemen."[11]

By 1834, a series of riots against the abolitionist movement and free Blacks flowed throughout Connecticut, New York, New Jersey, New Hampshire and South Carolina. Upheavals took place in Washington, D.C., Georgia, and Massachusetts as well. Even journalists had to be wary when they researched and reported their findings. Elijah Lovejoy, a minister and abolitionist, had his printing press destroyed and lost his life when a pro-slavery mob attacked his office in Illinois. Lovejoy's offense: the printing of a story on the mob lynching of a Black man that had taken place in the state.[12] Clearly taking sides at the federal level, in 1836 the U.S. House of Representatives enacted a gag rule banning the acceptance of petitions calling for the abolition of slavery. In essence, no matter where they landed on U.S. soil, the *La Amistad* captives would not have escaped the brewing battle over the presence of Black people, enslaved or free.

Even as the fractured movement against slavery struggled with internal philosophical differences, New York abolitionist Lewis Tappan galvanized resources to build a defensive circle around *La Amistad*'s imprisoned Africans. Tappan, along with his brother Arthur, belonged to a school of zealous white antislavery activists whose beliefs were steeped in religious faith. The two businessmen had an established record of using their wealth to support a broad spectrum of reform efforts. Having already focused on ridding the nation of strong drink and the pleasures of "fallen women," Lewis Tappan reached middle age before taking up the cause of abolishing slavery. Among the first to visit the jailed Africans, Tappan became a powerful voice arousing the disorganized and sometimes lethargic proponents of antislavery. Using the pages of the antislavery newspaper *The Emancipator* as his forum, he delivered running descriptions of his visits with the detained group.

In a letter to an antislavery friend in London, Tappan wrote of his fear that the U.S. government might attempt to simply give the Africans to the Spanish Government, "and we should be prepared for it,"[13] and prepare he did. Using his first visit with the prisoners to preach to them of his Christian faith, Tappan ascertained for himself that they could neither speak nor understand English and that they certainly knew nothing of his God. His next step was to join with two other abolitionists, Joshua Leavitt and Simeon Jocelyn, to form the "Amistad Committee."[14] The self-appointed trio sent out an appeal to "the friends of humanity," requesting funds to hire an interpreter to "secure able council for ... fellow men of Africa kidnapped, transported across the seas ... thrown upon our shores." Blacks and whites answered the call, giving out of pocket as well as organizing fundraising events.

Cincinnati's Colored Baptist Church raised what was then the enormous sum of $50.00.

As time approached for the first of what turned out to be several court trials, Tappan and the Amistad Committee prepared for a legal and publicity battle of national and international magnitude. The pivotal issue of the language barrier was addressed when the committee secured the services of Josiah Willard Gibbs and Thomas Gallaudet. Gibbs, a professor of linguistics at Yale University, and Gallaudet, who had created a sign language for the deaf, approached the problem as researchers. They soon determined that the captives spoke Mende, the language of Africans living in and around the British colony of Sierra Leone. Armed with this knowledge, Yale University students were enlisted to search the docks around New York City. Their mission successfully concluded when they located and enlisted the help of several African deckhands, three of whom were natives of the same general geographical area and similar language group as those aboard *La Amistad*.[15]

With the ability to communicate in something close to their native tongue, the captives offered their descriptions of what had happened. What emerged was a story of being forcibly taken from their homeland, placed aboard ships and subjected to a long journey at sea. Children, when finally acknowledged, told of being taken from their parents, brothers and sisters, whose names they easily remembered. With the assurance of Professor Gibbs that none could have been born in a Spanish-speaking language system, the development of a strong legal defense became the main priority. Although frequently presented as deranged religious zealots by their detractors, many whites who opposed slavery were politically astute. This was never more evident than in securing John Quincy Adams as the captives' legal counsel. In possession of more than oral eloquence, the respected lawyer had served as a member of the U.S. House of Representatives as well as

President of the United States. Opposed to slavery, Quincy's arguments before the Supreme Court rested on the fact that the slave trade had already been outlawed in both the U.S. and Spain. He included an additional line of reasoning that he was particularly qualified to address: the Spanish government was accused of attempting to circumvent the entire U.S. legal system by privately communicating with the executive office. His argument served to position the story of *La Amistad* as more than the rights of Africans on American shores; it morphed into a tale of behind-the-scenes political maneuvering that would threaten the rights of U.S. citizens. Adams' logic prevailed, and on March 9, 1841, the U.S. Supreme Court declared the captives neither slaves nor fugitives but free men. The court recognized that as Africans, they had been illegally and forcibly transported to U.S. waters and could not be prevented from returning to their home country. As they were free men, the killing of their captors was not murder, but self-preservation. The decision neither addressed nor had any legal effect on the United States' homegrown institution of slavery; neither did it suggest a means by which the foreign-born Blacks were to actually get back to their homeland.[16]

While the U.S. court system had legally changed the status of a specific group of Blacks from that of potential property to that of free men, the children aboard *La Amistad* appeared to exist in a somewhat nebulous category. Ruled by the court as witnesses to, but not participants in, the events that had taken place on the ship, they received minimal public attention during the trials. Lewis Tappan was one of a few to focus on the trauma suffered by the three girls, Te'me /Teme, Kag'ne and Mar'gru, as well as the boy Kali/Kale. Tappan, a father of five daughters and two sons, wrote compelling newspaper articles describing his visits with the young captives: "We went into a room ... to see the children. They were all sobbing aloud and appearing to be in great agony ... it was heart rending sight to see ... 4,000 miles from their parents and native land ... and no one able to converse with them, sooth [sic] their sorrows and quiet their fears." His concerns were not lessened when the children were brought into court and "placed at the bar." They "appeared to be in great affliction, and the girls wept exceedingly. The jailer stood by the side of them, offering them fruit to quite them, but they put it aside and refused to be comforted." Tappan believed that the children needed some form of legal guardianship "until matters are disposed of respecting them."[17] He would soon be proven right. Following the Supreme Court decision, Tappan and a few of his friends attempted to reunite the children with the other freed captives. Arriving at the home of the jailer where the children had been boarded, they were met with resistance. With the backing of a gathering mob, the jailer informed them that the children had become his own "domestic servants." In spite of the court order declaring them free, Tappan and his group had to force their way through a jeering mob to physically remove the young charges. When finally reunited with the other Africans at an abolitionist stronghold in Farmington, Connecticut, the girls were given new "Christian" names. Most likely in honor of Lewis Tappan's mother, Mar'gru was renamed Sarah, Kag'ne was given the name Charlotte, and Te'me became Maria Brown.[18]

Having followed the *La Amistad* case from its beginning, Black Americans were overjoyed that all of the Africans were finally freed. In articles read and shared across the country, the focus centered on the fact that Black men had fought for and won their freedom. Flowery editorials described the leader Cinque as "a noble hero" fit to join the ranks of "Patrick Henry, Thomas Jefferson...and other fathers of the American Revolution." Beyond noting that the age of the children appeared to be "7, 8 and 9," little attention was given to their presence.[19] In addition to celebrating the freedom of the *La Amistad* Captives, Black Americans joined in the pragmatic work that followed. Africans and free Blacks, as well as white abolitionists, all played a part in accumulating the resources required to outfit an ocean-worthy sailing vessel and crew. While being tutored in English and Christianity, the Africans made "native" trinkets and crafts that were sold. They also "raised a large quantity of corn, potatoes, onions ... which [would] ... be useful at sea." They raised funds by touring the Northeast along with interpreters, presenting their story to enthralled audiences of both Blacks and whites. In New York, hundreds of Black Americans willingly paid the large sum of $.50 per person in order to shake Cinque's hand. A half-century after the fact, one attendee remembered, "Frederick Douglass introduce[d] Cinquez .... I cannot forget or fail to feel the inspiration of that scene ... Cinquez ... had written his protest with the blood of his captors."[20] Four "largely Black" events in Philadelphia raised $400, while meetings held in New England's Black churches collected $1,000. Given the time period and the economic conditions facing free Black Americans, such sums represented an enormous sacrifice.[21] With the resources needed for the returnees slowly accumulating, and the Africans growing more anxious to begin their voyage home, one last tour was organized. Final departure ceremonies and fundraising events took place in late November 1841 in New York City.

Once freed, the Africans were of less interest to the general public, but the *Colored American* newspaper continued to provide coverage of the groups' public appearances. The Amistad committee was not disappointed, as large and sometimes tearful throngs filled the final three gatherings. At the First Colored Presbyterian Church, The Broadway Tabernacle, and The Zion African Methodist Church, crowds assembled to hear the group sing songs in their native language and retell the story of their capture. Newspapers recorded that Sarah Mar'gru, thought to be around 10 years old, contributed to the festivities with a reading of the 130th Psalm in English."[22]

On December 4, 1841, the captive children had the rare experience of reversing their journey across the ocean. Along with the surviving adults, they boarded a ship—*The Gentleman*—off of Staten Island, destined for Sierra Leone, Africa. They left behind a still-struggling movement against slavery along with Black Americans who festooned their homes and other gathering places with images of the ship *La Amistad*. The human face of the drama was, and has continued to be, that of Cinque, whose willingness to fight to gain his freedom secured his place as a true Black hero.[23] In addition to cloaking the Africans in heroic valor, there were some who believed "something should be done by *us* for the land our fathers loved." Sponsored by the Black Union Missionary Society, an African American couple, Henry and Tamar Wilson, answered the call and joined three white missionaries in the return trip to Sierra Leone.[24]

After more than seven weeks at sea, the returnees had almost come full circle. They set foot once again on the continent of Africa, but they had not yet returned "home." Disembarking at Freetown, Sierra Leone, in late January 1842, Mar'gru and her fellow sojourners had reached a "repatriation" zone in Africa. For more than 50 years this British ruled territory had been one in which the buying, selling, or owning of slaves was prohibited. In essence, Africans "displaced" as a result of the slave trade were "resettled" in Freetown. It housed an international population of Blacks including some from the slums of London, Jamaican Maroons and transplants from America. As far as Mar'gru had come, this slice of Africa ruled by the British and surrounded by several different indigenous tribal groups would not become her home.

Honoring their commitment to accompany the *La Amistad* returnees and spread Christianity into Africa, the missionaries and their wards left Freetown for the countryside.[25] Within months, on land loaned by or rented from a local chief, the rudimentary Mende (or Kaw Mende) Mission came to life.

The challenges of tribal warfare, cultural differences, and exposure to new diseases were complicated even more by internal struggles over the day-to-day leadership of the settlement. In spite of such difficulties, the missionaries continued their work under the assumption that the "returnees" would, without question, dedicate their lives to the mission. Having escaped enslavement in a foreign land, however, they had returned to Africa with ideas and concerns of their own.[26] In less than a year, most of those known to the world as the *La Amistad* captives began the process of reshaping their own lives. Even the mighty Cinque left the Mende mission in hopes of reuniting with the family he had not seen in more than two years. With fewer than 10 of the "rescued" men and three girls Kag'ne/Charlotte, Te'me/Maria and Mar'gru/Sarah, the band of missionaries continued their work.

It was soon apparent that Sarah/Mar'gru was the most capable of gathering the local natives to teach them to read. As her skills continued to develop, the missionaries' efforts to create a school for girls took root. With the idea that formal education would prepare Sarah Mar'gru to organize and lead the school, the American Missionary Society agreed to sponsor her return trip to the United States. At the approximate age of 14, Sarah was on a third voyage across the Atlantic. Along with another missionary, Eliza Raymond, Mar'gru returned to America in 1846 aboard the brig *Oriental.* Raymond, whose infant daughter had died of "fever" at the Mende Mission, was returning home in a state of both physical and mental exhaustion. In a reversal of fortunes, her young traveling companion entered a world open to few girls or women in the entirety of the world. Even the progressive Oberlin College in Ohio found a female student from Africa a new phenomenon. Finding herself once again essentially alone in a foreign country, Mar'gru confided in her old benefactor, Lewis Tappan, "I am now studying very diligently ... I am now rooming alone. This makes me think about home. Sometimes I feel low spirit[ed] and cry then ... Mr. Tappan, don't forget me for I look to you as a Father and if you forget me I don't know what I shall do."[27] For a time, Sarah shared a room with Lucy Stanton, a Black American student from Cleveland, Ohio.[28]

By the winter of 1848, Sarah had mastered college preparatory courses and moved on to the college level. She studied alongside a rare assortment of Black, white, male and female students.[29] Though not the only Black student at Oberlin to overcome near-impossible odds in attending college, Sarah was surely among the most exotic. Not only the sole African to be found on campus, she was also the only student who had garnered international recognition as one of the *La Amistad* captives. She also joined an extremely small cohort of Black female students who embarked on an "advanced" education prior to the Civil War. While their numbers remained comparatively low, and while many—including Sarah—had to perform domestic chores around the college to defray the cost of their education, Oberlin's young Black women exhibited a willingness to challenge boundaries. Arriving from families or communities that had been actively involved in antislavery and civil rights issues, most expected more from their education than the possibility of becoming silent and invisible "ladies." Without abandoning the notion of respectability, they were also acutely aware that the world held tight reins on both Blacks and women. College gave them a relatively safe opportunity to push against barriers determined to confine them by race and/or gender.

Although Oberlin College afforded students a privileged and sheltered environment, it did not and could not completely protect Black students from the facts of race on or off campus. But neither the president of the college nor the "Ladies Governing Board" could completely control the ideas and opinions of their dark-skinned charges.[30] Within this environment, Sarah Mar'gru seldom gave her benefactors reason to question their support. In addition to mastering courses in algebra, geography, Roman history, and philosophy, she was described as a good girl whose "conduct seems to be regulated by strictly religious principles." For the Christian-based anti-slavery movement, she was the perfect symbol. Her quick mastery of coursework and overall obedience caused one teacher to write: "shame on the man who will say a Negro cannot learn ... for he would surely be obliged to say that one at least of Africa's Sable Daughters can and does learn as rapidly as any of the fairer skin. And if one, why not more?"[31]

If, on the surface, Sarah Mar'gru's behavior called forth such praise, there was also evidence of another side to her personality. On different occasions she confided, "I ... would not stay in this country for a thousand dollars if it were not to get an education," and, "Africa is my home. I long to be there. Although I am in America yet my heart is there, the people I love and the country I admire."[32]

Glimmers of such independent thinking could only be seen by some of her benefactors as slight "faults."[33] One such "fault" may have been Sarah's affiliation with one of the more progressive student groups, the Female Moral Reform Society. Along with at least four other Black female students, Sarah joined the campus chapter of the organization. Under the umbrella of strengthening civic morality, women both on and off campus created organizations linked to broader reform movements of the period. Since "moral" reform included the fight against prostitution, alcohol and slavery, the Society boldly argued that men and women should be held equally accountable for their transgressions. More than simply opposing such behaviors, society members wanted to do something about it. In the years before Sarah's arrival at Oberlin, the Ohio State Chapter of the Female Moral Reform Society had collected enough petitions to lobby the legislature for a bill that would make adultery a crime punishable by law. The organization's New York chapter pledged to reform prostitutes but wanted to "penalize those who use or profit from it as well."[34] Associating with women who were intruding into male territories of sex, crime and politics was surely not what Sarah Mar'gru's benefactors had in mind when they sent her off to college.

Arguably the best indicator that a kidnapped African child was developing a small but independent sense of herself was a subtle but significant scrimmage over her name. Along with the other *La Amistad* captives, the child, Mar'gru, meaning "Black snake," had been renamed and returned to her homeland as "Sarah." In departing Sierra Leone for the second time, she sailed in pursuit of the rare gift of education, but once again she arrived on the shores of another continent entangled in issues of slavery. Stated most clearly by her devoted supporter, Lewis Tappan, Sarah was advised to continue using the name "Mar'gru." It would identify her, he reasoned, as one with links to *La Amistad*. Yet, in letters she subsequently wrote, Sarah rarely if ever used the name Mar'gru alone, preferring instead "Sarah Mar'gru" or "Sarah Kinson." Perhaps registering a bit of pique, she explained her use of the last name Kinson saying that she "was called by that name …. and is better known by it." Rather than expressing commitment to any particular cause or ideology, Sarah Mar'gru may have been trying to carve out a bit of her own space. For a young person who had literally been snatched away from her birth family and culture as a child to be violently dragged into an unimaginable foreign existence, the luxury of being able to express some preference in a name was no small thing. In a similar vein, Frederick Douglass also struggled to establish his own identity among his white supporters. Douglass, an eloquent and fiery speaker, complained about abolitionists who had advised him not to appear too intelligent and well-spoken, stating he was advised to "have a little of the plantation manner of speech … tis not best that you seem too learned."[35]

In spite of any discomfort, Sarah kept her supporters apprised of her life as a college student. Focusing on her studies, she wrote of taking courses in the "history of England and Comstock's Philosophy." While considering courses in botany and astronomy, it was mathematics that she "liked best." Her correspondence also clearly revealed her desire to return home to Sierra Leone. Anticipating her journey, she wrote, "I am so glad that I am going home next fall. I can hardly wait for the time to come. Will you write and let me know when I shall go home ... I think I must go home next fall if you wish me to do any good among my country people."[36]

This longing to return home was coupled with a desire to remain at Oberlin to "take up" more studies that would "benefit [her] ... very much." The push and pull between Africa and Oberlin was exacerbated by news that, back home, the Kaw Mende Mission had suffered more deaths. First, Mr. Raymond, the Oberlin missionary who had accompanied the returnees back to Sierra Leone, and then Kag'ne/Charlotte, "one of my fellow prisoners" had succumbed to "fever." More than just a fellow captive, Kag'ne had been Sarah Mar'gru's closest contact and a constant comfort aboard *La Amistad* and after. Bonded by their shared experience, she had become a sister who "used to tell us that one day we shall see our native land."[37]

After more than three years in the United States, Sarah was again boarding a ship to cross the Atlantic Ocean. Arriving once more in Freetown, Sierra Leone, in November of 1849, she returned a changed person; no longer a child but a young woman prepared to lead a girls school at the Kaw Mende mission. As she was still unable to locate her own family, the mission and its inhabitants remained the center of her world, but that also emphasized her own dislocation. The Kaw Mende Mission School was essentially a neutral U.S. outpost situated between warring African territories, some of which had been partially colonized by the British. On a day-to-day basis,

Sarah had to negotiate a world composed of native Africans, American whites and the occasional African American. Differences within, as well as between, each group demanded highly sophisticated survival skills. For example, among the white Americans was William Brown, who had come to Africa from a Southern U.S. slaveholding background. Staunchly opposed to Blacks serving as missionaries in Africa, Brown held a sacred belief that natives only held respect for white men. Using cruelty, Brown garnered the "respect" he was due. And then there was Hannah More, one of the few American women at the mission, whose letters to America detailed her suffering a lack of available friendship with other white women.[38] For native Africans, Sarah Mar'gru and her story could only be thought of as akin to fable.

Within this unsettled world, the meaning of home, family and even companionship was stretched to embrace new forms for Sarah Mar'gru. In a letter to Lewis Tappan, still her stalwart supporter back in the U.S., one can hear the voice of both an abandoned child and a young woman struggling to make a life for herself in a foreign place called home:

> Mr. Raymond is dead and I have no one to look to but you. He was a father to me. He was such a good father that I hardly ever think of my own parents ... I expect to have a house soon and I shall have nothing to put in it. Do Mr. Tappan help me if you please. In this Mission we have to buy everything even plate, spoon, knife, and everything for a woman to keep a house ... I want you to send me a bed and things to keep a house for I expect to have a house soon and I shall have Nothing to put in it.[39]

It is much too easy to view such a request as evidence of an acquired thirst for material goods or items from the United States. More charitably, it can be understood as Sarah's desire to create her own permanent dwelling space. Sarah Mar'gru Kinson had survived most of her life in various temporary and sometimes unthinkable substitutes for "home." Forcibly removed from her family, she had occupied space as property or cargo aboard slave ships and in a foreign jail. With the help of abolitionists, she then found herself sheltered in a series of dwellings offered by benevolent strangers whose language she had to learn to speak. Oberlin College had provided quarters with various students and teachers as well as a solitary room of her own. In Sierra Leone, home and work took place on the grounds of a mission school, but here she lived among others deeply immersed in their own sense of displacement. In fact, there had been no real home since Sarah Mar'gru had been taken from her parents. It is little wonder that she was ready to fashion a space and a life of her own.

By 1852 at approximately 20 years of age—less than 15 years from the start of her journey on the slave ship *La Amistad*—Sarah Mar'gru Kinson was beginning to steer her own course. After a failed engagement to an older African man of whom little is known, Sarah finally began married life with another teacher, Edward Henry Green. Green, an African and a recent convert to Christianity, had been educated in a British Mission school in Freetown. They were wed in September of 1852 and both continued to work at the mission. Two years later, Sarah Mar'gru got closure on another important issue. Under her signature of "Mrs. Sarah Green" she wrote to Lewis Tappan, "I found my father, he is very far off from the Mission, about a weeks journey, but he heard of me, that I am yet living, only the war have hindered him from coming. But the war is now at an end so he send some men to see me and they have returned to him to tell him that I am alive yet. I am not able to express my thanks to the Almighty for his goodness to me."[40]

Although it is uncertain if father and daughter ever saw one other again, Sarah Mar'gru embarked on the last documented phase of her life. In 1855, she and her husband left the Kaw Mende settlement to set up another station of the mission further into the interior. It is at this point that reports on her life become less reliable. For a time, there was communication between the new outpost and Kaw Mende mission, but slowly that trickled to an end, and Mar'gru Sarah Kinson Green faded back into the land of her birth. More than simply surviving, she had lived an extraordinary life, yet she remains little more than a small figure orbiting great men and powerful social movements of her time. While events surrounding her life have been etched into state, national, and international history, it is easy to understand why a child with memories of the slave ship *La Amistad* grew up with a fear of "being forgotten." Written in 1854, one of her last letters on record contains her oft-repeated plea: "is my name forgotten …. Am I not a sister in Christ …?"[41] During her recorded lifetime, Sarah Mar'gru was exposed to, endured and survived a set of experiences known to few of her race, age and gender. She left behind an extraordinary study of both trauma and resilience, neither of which should be forgotten. But even as she receded into the pages of undocumented history, another young Black woman was moving onto the stage.

Chapter Two

Sarah Parker Remond: From Salem, Massachusetts, to The British Isles "Like Hot Lead to Pour on the Americans"

As the ties between Sarah Mar'gru in Sierra Leone and her friends in America first frayed and finally were severed, another vastly different Sarah was finding her own reasons to cross the Atlantic. Governed by circumstances vastly different from those that had controlled Sarah Mar'gru, Sarah Parker Remond traveled not as cargo aboard a slave ship, but as a paying passenger on a steamship. In 1859, Remond made her way from America to England in order to "gather up polite sentiment and pour it like hot lead on the Americans."[1] Attempting such a voyage to place her ideas on public display would have been unusual for any woman in the nineteenth century, but a Black woman doing so before audiences in Europe was a true curiosity. The trajectory of Sarah Remond's life as a third-generation freewoman calling a nation to judgment on an international stage demands serious attention.

Perhaps the most important factor shaping Sarah Parker Remond's life was the accident of birth into a free and financially secure Black family in Salem, Massachusetts. Black Salem was a small but vibrant community, and the federal census of 1790 listed none of its residents as slaves. Increasing slowly, the Black residential population was estimated at 282 in 1837, most of whom lived within a "colored" enclave. A seaport town, Salem featured a shipping industry that provided employment on the wharves, with a few Black men signing on ships as sailors. Others were involved in service occupations as gardeners, chimney sweeps and stable hands. Women and children could find jobs in household service and as cooks. A particularly unusual profession was held by Chloe Minns, who was hired in 1807 as a teacher for Black children, a position she held for nearly two decades.[2] Although freed from the scourge of slavery, Blacks were not integrated into Salem communities. In the first decades of the nineteenth century, racial separation, sometimes benign but always present, was the norm in every aspect of life. Black men and women formed their own societies and organizations, holding public functions sometimes in conjunction or competition with the more populous Boston just a few miles away. In the early 1770s, along with other Black New Englanders, those in Salem adopted the practice of gathering for an annual festival to elect their own "governor," or ruler.[3]

Social activities did not supplant or prevent agitation for equal rights; in fact, a campaign for integrated public facilities was underway before 1840. Education was a major focal point in the overall push for full citizenship rights. In collaboration with white reformers, the Black New Englanders lobbied politicians, boycotted Black schools and mounted petition drives protesting separate and unequal treatment. In April 1855, the Massachusetts state legislature signed a bill making it the first state in the country to outlaw racial segregation in schools, a right that citizens of Salem had been demanding for over a decade.[4]

This was the broader community into which Sarah Parker Remond was born. As the ninth child in a family of well-to-do African Americans, Sarah was an anomaly to most Blacks and all whites, but the Remond family had been born of unusual circumstances. In 1798, John Remond's mother sent him from the Southern Caribbean island of Curaçao, up the Atlantic Coast to America. The future Remond family patriarch arrived in America a free Black immigrant child under the protection of a ship captain. He had few, if any, immediate connections to the African American community. Making his way to Boston, he learned the trades of barbering and catering. In 1807, John's marriage to Nancy Lenox added the crucial element of citizenship to the lives of their future descendants. As a matriarch, she provided incontestable American roots and clear expectations of full citizenship rights. Lenox had grown up in a large, free Black family of moderate but stable comfort. Her own father, Cornelius Lenox, had fought in the Revolutionary Army, and by 1800 had become a tax-paying free-holder in the town of Newton, Massachusetts. His children, including Nancy, were all educated in trades customary for free Blacks of the period, with the expectation that they would all join him in the family-owned hairdressing salon. While the boys trained as barbers, their sister Nancy was sent to Boston to learn catering and fancy food preparation. It was a skill that would bring her economic stability, as well as a measure of public recognition. An advertisement in an 1849 issue of the *Salem Gazette* suggests an assertive businesswoman soliciting "a share of public patronage" for "cakes of various kinds made to order." She also served "mock-turtle soup, venison … and some times ducks."[5] After her marriage to John Remond, Nancy Lenox embarked upon a life that was in many ways typical for nineteenth century women. Giving birth 10 times between 1809 and 1826, she led a life that was centered, out of necessity, on her family.[6] It was, however, a family life that included her involvement in the public arena. The Remonds, much like other free Blacks in the North, could not afford or did not choose to secret women behind closed doors.

By 1824 and the birth of their daughter Sarah, the Remonds were a well-entrenched family of Massachusetts entrepreneurs. Serving prepared food from the back door of their living quarters, as well as catering gatherings for the wealthy, the growing family expanded its business to take advantage of other opportunities as well. Undoubtedly, it was the skill of a spouse trained in fancy food preparation that allowed

John Remond, also trained in catering, to boastfully advertise in a Salem newspaper. Customers were promised delivery of oysters anywhere in Salem cooked to satisfaction and guaranteed to arrive hot.[7] It is little wonder that, as an adult, Sarah Remond remembered her mother as having "indomitable energy," bearing responsibility for training all her children to "the habits of industry."[8] With a foothold in food preparation, the family also began to supply ship and local merchants with a variety of foodstuffs. The amazing array of items included ham from Virginia, smoked beef from Albany, cigars from Spain, wine from Lisbon and soy from India.[9]

Residing in one of the largest seaport towns in the country, coupled with family economic involvement in trade, shaped Sarah Remond's early development. More than for most Americans, the trappings of that which was "foreign" were intricately woven into the Remond family life and livelihood. At one end of the spectrum was a world that Sarah understood as larger than her immediate physical surroundings. At the other end was the day-to-day reality of Black life in America, where "even those coloured people who were free were only nominally so, except in Massachusetts; and even there their due rights were obtained by supernatural efforts."[10]

Of all the Remond children, Sarah was the only one who did not find her niche in any family enterprise. In a clan in which "every member of the family was expected to contribute a share toward the general whole," her siblings developed a network of businesses, some of which were passed on to a third generation. Working alongside her mother until her late twenties, Sarah seemed only passively involved in the economic ventures or antislavery activities occupying a large part of the Remond family life.[11]

Among free Blacks of the North, Black women's involvement in abolition and racial progress efforts were expected and indeed depended on as the norm. As Black men organized, joined and supported a wide range of African American integrated, antislavery and racial-uplift efforts, women were involved in comparable "female" efforts. Most understood and worked within the boundary lines described by escaped slave-turned-abolitionist William Wells Brown:

> [S]ewing circles will have a salutary effect upon all. Nothing looks more cheering to me than to see a circle of women working with their own hands for the redemption of their enslaved countrymen .... And why should they not labor for the downfall of slavery? Are not more than a million of females driven daily to the sugar, the cotton, the rice and tobacco plantations of the south? Are they not denied the marriage rite.[12]

Given the gender conventions and race restrictions of the day, the space that Black women carved out for themselves was remarkable. Indeed, it was perhaps just this position that pushed Salem's women of color to organize America's first female antislavery society in 1832. Using sewing circles, bazaars and church societies, they mapped out their own complementary agenda directed toward freeing slaves, acquiring equal rights and establishing "racial uplift." The efforts benefiting from their work included the antislavery press, abolitionist lecturers and support for runaway slaves.[13] While women of the Remond clan occupied leadership positions in Salem's women's antislavery movement, Sarah's interest can be measured primarily by attendance at antislavery lectures.[14] It was not until 1853, at the age of 27, that Sarah Remond began to show signs of just how much she had absorbed. Particularly close to her brother Charles, she would attempt to emulate his style of public confrontation. Unlike other members of the family, Charles Remond had committed himself to the unpredictable and dangerous life of a professional abolitionist. Preceding Frederick Douglass, Charles reigned as the first and most eloquent Black abolitionist lecturer appointed by the Massachusetts Anti-Slavery Society. Giving voice to the increasingly independent and more militant Black agenda, Charles Remond warned Blacks that "we need more radicalism among us ... we are too indefinite in views and sentiment ... too slow in movements."[15] As a delegate to the World Anti-Slavery Convention in London, 1840, he acted on such beliefs. Charles Remond, along with William Lloyd Garrison, protested the exclusion of women from the conference floor by joining them in the balcony. It was an act that William Lloyd Garrison later described as having "done more to bring up for the consideration of Europe the rights of women than could have been accomplished in any other manner."[16] In accounting for his own actions, Charles Remond responded directly: "In the name of heaven, and in the name of the bleeding, dying slave, I ask if I shall scruple the propriety of female action, of whatever kind or description. I trust not—I hope not—I pray not."[17]

Just as Charles had taken a seat in the balcony to protest the treatment of women in the fight against slavery, Sarah Remond tested the waters of her convictions in a similar fashion. In defiance of established custom (if not law), Sarah, along with her younger sister Caroline, refused to accept seating in the Black gallery section of a Boston theater. After demanding seating on the main floor reserved for whites, for which they had bought tickets, Sarah and Caroline were forcibly removed from the theater.

Within months of winning the subsequent lawsuit they filed, Sarah Remond involved herself in another incident in Philadelphia. This time, Sarah and two friends were ejected from an exhibition hall after being accused of not having purchased tickets. On this occasion, the lawsuit filed by another member of the group was not successful, but for Sarah, a corner had nonetheless been turned.

Treating the inevitable reality of racial prejudice as a frustrating fact of life, Black women chose more than one way of negotiating the terrain outside of their homes. Though Remond women were not expected to court physical confrontation, it was not assumed that they should or would silently accept ill treatment. When refused service in a Philadelphia ice cream establishment, Sarah's youngest sister, Caroline, "told one of the people some wholesome truths, which cannot be soon forgotten." When ordered into a "colored car" on another occasion, Caroline once again "indignantly refused to do so and was obliged to return home and wait for the 10 o'clock ... in which she had no difficulty."[18] In an increasingly escalating pattern, Sarah and Caroline's behavior moved well beyond the customary range of conduct for female resistance. Sarah continued to carve out her own direction. Once again with encouragement from her brother Charles, Sarah joined him as an antislavery lecturer. By the end of 1856, she was honing her skills with lectures in New York, Ohio, Massachusetts, Pennsylvania and Canada. Joining the American Anti-Slavery Society, Sarah was elected one of the association's vice presidents. She served on the finance committee alongside Susan B. Anthony.[19] By the end of 1858, with improved speaking skills and an enlarged appetite, Remond admitted to "an intense desire to visit England, that I might for a time enjoy freedom." Without severing ties with the antislavery society, she proceeded with her own plans, going forth "on her own responsibility, not representing any society."[20]

Remond's choice of England as a destination was based on more than uninformed longings. For decades, Great Britain had enjoyed the reputation of being open to reformers, radicals and exiles. London itself had become both a temporary destination and home to "Poles escaping repression following the Cracow uprising of 1846, Italian proletarians, Turks, Russians, Scandinavians, and Dutch." Welcoming professional abolitionists, Blacks escaping slavery and others seeking educational or professional opportunities denied in their own homeland helped to solidify Great Britain's image as "the moral arbiter of the western world"; however, at least one American visitor was not impressed by such accolades. Describing herself as "a coloured female preacher," Zilphas Elaw did not consider London a moral paradise. Spending her first Sunday "in the metropolis of the most Christian country in the world ... much surprised to see the shops open, and many kinds of business in the course of transaction, women crying fruits for sale, and the people intent on traffic and marketing." Elaw lived in England for five years, convinced that her ministry was a "blessing to hundreds of persons ... living in sin and darkness before they saw my coloured face."[21]

By the early 1850s, the list of Black Americans making their way to Great Britain included both Frederick Douglass and Sarah's beloved brother Charles Lenox Remond. Something approximating a transatlantic propaganda machine had evolved as Black Americans resolved to draw global attention to their plight and build opposition against slavery. Working both as free agents and with various factions of the British antislavery movement, Frederick Douglass and Charles Remond carved out a place for themselves as leaders of an international movement.[22] This was the environment in which Sarah Remond chose to envelop herself.

Her arrival in Liverpool in January 1859 coincided with an important juncture in the antislavery movement. While the flow of Blacks across the Atlantic had slowed to a trickle, women's involvement in the British antislavery movement had begun to pick up the pace; it formed a part of the larger campaign for women's rights.[23] Even within this environment, Sarah represented a rare experience for the British public. Unlike the infamous Frederick Douglass, Remond was not the charismatic fugitive slave, nor could she be mistaken for other Black women already known to the British public. In contrast with Mary Prince, Ellen Craft or Harriet Jacobs, she was a free-born Black American woman; neither her parents nor grandparents had been enslaved.[24] With the prevailing image of Black women as hapless victims, few Europeans had exposure to other representations. Indeed, by 1828, the dominating symbol of the British antislavery campaign was that of a kneeling slave woman with clasped hands, her wrists encircled in chains. Sarah Remond was a real-life response to the motto's implied question surrounding the visual image, "Am I not a woman and a sister."[25] Here was, in fact, a Black American woman whose life and personal agenda brought to the surface questions that lay at the convergence of beliefs about race, class and gender. In pursuit of her own agenda, Sarah Parker Remond ultimately became the first woman to speak to the issues of slavery before mass audiences in Great Britain.[26]

In spite of the lingering side effects Remond experienced as a result of a rough transatlantic crossing, her first lecture in Liverpool, in January of 1859, was rapidly followed by many others. Credited with pumping new life into a flagging movement in Warrington, England, she made three appearances between January 24 and February 2 of that year. Sarah was rewarded with contributions for the coffers of the American Anti-Slavery Society and more than 3,000 signatures on a petition condemning slavery in America.[27] During the following two years, both as a lone speaker and by joining with other reform lecturers, Remond established her reputation. The prospect of hearing a Black woman deliver a public lecture undoubtedly helped to attract overflowing crowds in London, Manchester and Leeds. In Bury, Remond held forth "with hundreds of persons seeking in vain to gain admission." In Ireland and Scotland the press recorded equally large crowds who had gathered to hear and see "a native of a village near Boston."[28]

As she was an agent for no specific organization, Sarah crafted and delivered her own message. At the center of her discourse was a double-edged attack on the illegal and unconstitutional nature of slavery in America and the specific sufferings of slave women. In no uncertain terms, she took to task ministers of the gospel and politicians of the South. Theirs were sins accomplished with the aid of "northern states where slavery did not exist." English men and women were asked to "send forth ... indignant protest against this glaring system." As bold as her attacks were on the political systems and on the powerful men of America, a far more perilous topic was the "degradation" women dare not mention.[29] Described by the press as possessing "womanly dignity" and accepted by the ladies of Warrington as a sister, Sarah called attention to the suffering of sisters not so fortunate as those gathered before her. As she intruded into the public space reserved for men, Sarah Remond risked scorn by including the specifics of female enslavement. Painting scenes of an "open market place" where "women are exposed for sale ... their persons not always covered," Sarah warned English men and woman that women "are sold into slavery with cheeks like the lily and the rose, as well as those that might compare with the wing of a raven." Employing the image of slaves with skin as white as any in her audience, the "gifted lady from across the Atlantic" pointed out that "the more Anglo-Saxon blood ... the more gold is poured out when the auctioneer has a woman for sale, because they are sold to be concubines for white Americans."[30] Calling forth the lives of fictional characters as well as those such as Margaret Garner, an escaped slave mother who had taken the life of her child to prevent recapture, Remond discreetly called attention to those who "suffered greatest" under slavery.[31]

With antislavery lecturing as the grounding force in her life, Remond began to pursue the second goal that had pulled her across the Atlantic. By October of 1859, settled in London, she was entrenched in a community of women social reformers and was taking courses at Bedford College for Women.[32] A strong network of antislavery women provided Remond with both a surrogate family and political kindred spirits. By 1860, Remond had begun to study nursing while continuing to lecture as an agent for the Leeds Young Men's Anti-Slavery Society. Later that year and into the next, she lectured throughout Scotland.[33]

By 1861, as Northern forces fired on Fort Sumter, signaling the start of the War Between the States, Remond's strong ideological differences and personal distaste for her homeland shaped her response. She predicted the only road to emancipation was "a great shedding of blood." Her sole remorse was for the slaves "who the South could not keep and the North did not want."[34] This pointed reference to the nebulous state of the future for Blacks in America was reflected among the British as well. An official governmental declaration of neutrality did not curtail continuous discussion in the public and political arena. Summing up a broad range of reactions, Sarah applied her energies directly to what she saw as fear and weakness among the British. She advised, "Let not diplomacy of statesmen, no intimidation of slave holder's, no scarcity of cotton, no fear of slave insurrection, prevent the people of Great Britain from maintaining their position as the friend of the oppressed Negro; which they deservedly occupied previous to the disastrous Civil War."[35] Dispatching with the very real problem of a textile industry intricately tied to slave-produced cotton, she directed an overflow crowd of 600 gathered in Edinburgh to consider "cotton from India."[36]

As the war continued, Remond's lectures were supplemented with more concrete forms of action. She supported the American antislavery press by forwarding a "mite" to assist William Lloyd Garrison with his newspaper, *The Liberator*.[37] Joining the Ladies' London Emancipation Society in its effort to educate the public and garner support for newly freed Blacks, Remond assembled one of the association's tracts.[38] As the title suggests, she designed "The Negro Anglo Africans as Freedmen and Soldier" to present Black Americans as active participants in the struggle to end slavery; as such, they were worthy of support. With the use of reports from the U.S. Secretary of War, Remond called attention to the needs of both Black and white refugees. As the war progressed, whites, some of whom were British, had been trapped in the midst of battle.[39] Such information became an important weapon in efforts to steel British hearts and minds against pro-Confederate sympathies. Indeed, the war progressed alongside a discernible wave of anti-Black feeling within the British population. In the past, Blacks in the United Kingdom had experienced little of the direct and open hostility that was a part of daily life in the United States. In the decade leading up to the war, however, a discernible shift began to take place. By 1860, Frederick Douglass, whose "purchase price" had been paid by an English abolitionist, had cause to warn British humanitarians of a growing tide of racism among their countrymen.[40] A few years later, Douglass' concerns were corroborated by William Craft, who had also escaped slavery and was living in London. In 1863, Craft forced a session of the British Association for the Advancement of Science to adjourn early when he challenged papers delivered by two leading social scientists. John Crawford and James Hunt, both officers of the Anthropological Society of London, presented research pointing out differences between the Negro and the European. In both papers, the conclusions placed Europeans in the position of superiority while the "pure negro" was deemed incapable of "advances further in intellect than an intelligent European boy of fourteen." Conference members were asked to accept further "evidence" arguing that Negroes and Europeans were two distinct species. In responding to the papers, William Craft exhibited both humor and calm indignation. Pointing to differences in skin color between southern and northern Europeans, Craft asked the audience to consider "that climate had a tendency to bleach as well as to blacken. The thickness of the skull of the Negro had been wisely arranged by Providence to defend the brain from the tropical climate in which he lived. If god had not given them thick skulls their brains would probably have become very much like many scientific gentlemen of the present day."[41]

By 1865, ideas and beliefs about race were undoubtedly fueled by events that struck closer to home than the prospects and possibilities of newly freed Blacks in America. Reacting to a Black uprising protesting cruel treatment in British Jamaica, colonial authorities responded with full military might. Before order was restored, more than 400 Blacks were executed, hundreds of women and children were flogged and more than 1,000 homes were deliberately destroyed. For much of the English public, the slaughter was reduced to images of mindless Black savages lusting for the blood of whites. It was not a far leap to acceptance of the uprising as proof that Blacks were unfit for life as free people. An English newspaper advised that American legislators would do well to "keep in mind the sad past and present misery of Jamaica."[42]

In the years that had passed since Sarah had come to England in search of "a little freedom," she, like most of her countrymen, had chosen to overlook racial incidents or at least to not publicly criticize her host country. Whatever indignities endured abroad by African Americans, they compared weakly to the treatment suffered by Blacks in America. Determined to keep the focus on Blacks in the United States, most shared Frederick Douglass' sentiments. In describing a visit to Eaton Hall, Douglass informed the antislavery press in America that "the statuary did not fall down, the pictures did not leap from their places, the door did not refuse to open, and the servants did not say 'we don't allow niggers in here.'"[43]

In the aftermath of the Jamaican uprising, Sarah found reason to include Britain in her unrelenting attack on racial hatred. With British newspapers generally supporting the actions of the military in defending English honor in Jamaica, Sarah responded with her own letter to the *London Daily*

News. The tone of the letter reveals a level of disappointment and outrage previously reserved for the United States. Without equivocating, Remond opened her letter by declaring she did not accept as true "all the cruelties reported during the recent insurrection." In the words that followed, Sarah linked the treatment of Blacks in Jamaica to that of Blacks in America. Charging the British public with "a change in opinion ... in reference to the colored race," they had become indistinguishable from "any Southern Confederate or negro hating Northerner." Readers were challenged to compare reported charges of Black savagery in Jamaica to the Southerners in America who, "for eight generations have mutilated their slaves, and not infrequently during the present generation burnt their victims to death ... notch the ears of men and women, cut pleasant poesies in their shrinking flesh, learn to write with pens of red-hot iron on human face."[44]

For Sarah Parker Remond, England, the place that had once offered her safety had come to resemble America so closely that it could no longer serve as her real or imagined refuge. Ignoring suggestions that she belonged "in the midst of the emancipated negroes, nursing the wounded or educating the others," Sarah, as always, began to chart her own course.[45] Leaving London on August 10, 1866, she traveled first to Switzerland and then to her destination in Italy. Giving little information as to why she made this specific plan of action, it is nonetheless clear that this was not a decision based on a whim. Remond was now a woman who had proven her ability to survive alone outside of the confines of the United States. Life as a Black abolitionist abroad had placed her in contact with various reform causes and individuals. Indeed, by November of 1866, Remond would almost casually write to friends in America, "I had a very interesting interview with General Garibaldi last week. He is a true friend of the colored race and liberty everywhere."[46] Remond had also met another Italian revolutionary, Giuseppe Mazzini. Mazzini, a leading force in the fight for an independent and unified Italian kingdom, envisioned a broad movement that "respected no boundaries with workers, women, peasants, serfs, and slaves … among its beneficiaries."[47] Long before Sarah's arrival in England, Mazzini had spent decades in unrepentant political exile, but still retained influence in his own homeland. That Mazzini admired the white American radical abolitionist, John Brown, would undoubtedly have earned Sarah's interest as a kindred spirit. She would have also understood Italy as a destination not without its own challenges; nonetheless, she went about describing her movements in the language of a vacation travelogue. Readers of the National Anti-Slavery Standard were entertained with descriptions of her voyage to Italy. She wrote that "glorious mountain scenery … must be seen to be appreciated …. Lugano looked somber in the moonlight …. Garibaldians in their bright red shirts and caps …. A most becoming dress for an Italian. They are very handsome men."

As she made her way toward "the brightest and fairest land" she had ever looked upon, Sarah's letters did not avoid the darker side. In what can easily be read as a farewell letter to America, Sarah Remond also embraces "a sadder topic … 'the difficulties of reconstruction.'" With a clear-eyed assessment of the power that slavery had exercised in shaping American culture and institutions, Sarah predicted, "the hatred of race … is now the ruling element …. No one who really comprehended the terrible influence which for so many generations has corrupted the moral sense of the people, ever supposed that the contaminating influence of the system would be readily effaced …. What a record could the victims of this terrible hatred present against the dominate race …. It never will be written. It never can be written." The choice of language used in Sarah's correspondence has a clear tone of final separation: "May the colored race receive a fresh increase of the power to endure and bear, with such patience as they can command, fresh insults and injustice …. May God and their Integrity keep them in this new conflict."[48] Assigning the fate of Black Americans to a higher power and to their own devices, at forty years of age, Sarah Remond continued the work of creating a life of her own design. As if quoting an earlier Sarah Mar'gru, Remond was "uncertain how long I shall remain in Florence … I am not here for pleasure, but for study."[49]

And study is exactly what Sarah Remond did. By 1870, Remond listed her occupation in the Italian census as that of a physician.[50] The young woman who had once been disparagingly described by white abolitionists in America as having "manners and ways … peculiar to her race … and not in the least like the pretty one we saw at the New England convention," had come into her own. Those who had stood in judgment now confronted a mature woman fit to serve as an example to others. When antislavery activist Elizabeth Buffum Chase visited Florence in 1873, she returned to America with descriptions of "a remarkable woman … with a fine position in Florence as a physician." Chase included a compliment not imaginable in America: "If one tenth of the American women who travel in Europe were as noble and elegant as she is we shouldn't have to blush for our countrywomen as often as we do."[51] It was in Italy in the final decades of her life that Sarah Remond came closest to living the life that she desired as a free and independent woman. Once established in Italy, some aspects of her life took on the veneer of a typical, privileged European woman. Beneath that surface, and at her center, was an extraordinary Black American woman who had chosen exile over inequality. This in turn gave even her social life its own particular nuance. A broad array of Remond's visitors included English abolitionist William Robson, and Americans Lucy Chace and Frederick Douglass. Visiting artists included Black American sculptor Edmonia Lewis as well as Anne Whitney, a white sculptor from Massachusetts.[52] In 1877, Sarah Parker Remond's personal life took one more unexpected turn. She embarked upon a short-lived marriage to Lazario Pintor, a native of Sardinia. This was followed by a period of not-so-genteel poverty. Within two years, Pintor seemed to have disappeared from her life.[53] By 1885, Sarah's family in Italy had expanded to include more Remonds from America. A scarcity of records makes it difficult to determine the exact relationship that now existed between Sarah and the larger, extended Remond clan. Whatever the nature of that relationship, it was most likely maintained through her sister Caroline.

As early as 1859, just months after Sarah's initial arrival in England, Caroline, a young widow of independent means, had made the first of a series of visits to Europe. As Caroline's business partner, her unmarried sister Maritche Juan remained in Massachusetts in charge of their lucrative business ventures.[54] By 1885, as life for Blacks in America became increasingly defined by the rules of discrimination and inequality, both Caroline and Maritche Juan joined Sarah to take up residence in Rome. Describing an earlier visit to their home, Palazzo Maroni, Frederick Douglass noted, "Like myself, the Remond sisters—there was a third in Rome as well—with the exception of Caroline have grown quite old but in all of them I saw much of the fire of their eloquent brother Charles."[55]

In her own search for freedom and equal rights, Sarah Parker Remond proved to be more like her father than even John Remond himself might have expected. Decades after his own voyage up the Atlantic coast, from the island of Curaçao to America, his daughters extended the pattern. With Sarah in the lead, they became transatlantic voyagers who made lives for themselves on yet another continent. Like her mother, Sarah Remond had secured a means of providing for herself economically. Unlike her mother, she remained childless, but was in the end still surrounded by family. At the age of 70, having lived by the dictates of her own desires, Sarah Parker Remond died of undisclosed causes on December 13, 1894. She is buried in the Protestant cemetery in Rome.

Chapter Three

Anna Julia Cooper: Answering The Call of "A Thumping From Within"

Born between 1858 and 1860, Anna Julia Haywood Cooper's life bore little resemblance to that of either Mar'gru Sarah Kinson's or Sarah Parker Remond's. While Mar'gru had survived the transatlantic passage to return to Africa and neither Remond nor her parents had ever been enslaved, Anna Julia was born into a solidly entrenched system of human bondage. In spite of her beginnings, Anna spent a lifetime pushing against the forces that attempted to narrow her life choices. Living for more than 100 years, she unashamedly described her younger self as "an ambitious girl with a thumping from within unanswered by any beckoning from without."[1] It was that sense of internal certitude that led her to cross the Atlantic several times.

Coming into the world that was Raleigh, North Carolina, just a few years before the Civil War, Anna Julia Haywood spent her childhood immersed in the chaos of impending and actual war. Her home state was the site of nearly a dozen battles and accounted for more losses than any in the Confederacy. While bondage itself provided no safe haven for Black children, war and its aftermath offered even less security. For children as well as adults, day-to-day survival depended on an ability to negotiate the challenging transition between absolute servitude and yet-to-be-defined freedom.[2] As an adult, Cooper recalled being part of a slave "superstition," in which a newly awakened child was asked, "Which side is goin' to win de war? Will the Yankees beat de Rebs and will Linkum free de Niggers?" Having served as a young oracle in one such ritual herself, Cooper disclaimed the possession of any particular "vision or second sight" that might have been useful to herself or other troubled souls; however, the course of her subsequent life and work might suggest otherwise.[3]

Little "Annie Haywood" was the youngest child and only girl in her family. Her much-elder brother Rufus was born around 1836, with a second brother, Andrew, following in 1848. The center of this small family unit was a slave woman, Hannah Stanley Haywood, born in 1817. As might be expected, the question of who had fathered Hannah's children has remained open to discussion, but for Anna Cooper herself, this was a matter rarely and disdainfully remarked upon. She consistently described her biological father as "white ... and to who[m] I owe no indebtedness ... beyond the fact of my existence." On another occasion, while praising her mother, Anna divulged a bit more information: "Presumably my father was [mother's] master, if so I owe him not a sou." While the owner of the plantation on which Anna was born was Fabius J. Haywood, early researchers have suggested that a lawyer, George W. Haywood, was possibly her father. In 1934, her assumption was confirmed by a member of the Haywood family.[4]

While Anna Cooper expressed minimal interest in her paternal lineage, she loved and admired her mother. As a slave, Hannah Stanley had been forced to endure forms of exploitation that left her "too shame faced and modest ever to mention."[5] However, a mother's silence may have planted seeds that loosened her daughter's tongue. Published in 1892, Anna Cooper's book *A Voice From The South By A Black Woman of the South* is replete with references to "the hitherto voiceless Black Woman of America."

Even as her own education, research and writing provided entry to a wider world, Cooper continued to hear the "muffled ... mute ... and voiceless note of the sadly expectant Black Woman." In an era that clearly demanded otherwise, Cooper never strayed from her belief that "woman's strongest vindication for speaking is that the world needs to hear her voice."[6]

Even as she drew attention to the universal silencing of Black women, Anna Cooper continued to pay respect to her all-but-invisible mother. Disdain for the man who had fathered her did not lessen with time. Well into her sixties, Cooper wrote, "I owe nothing to my white father beyond the initial act of procreation. My mother's self-sacrificing toil to give me advantages she had never enjoyed is worthy of the highest praise and undying gratitude." By the 1930s, when her commitment to honor her mother led to the creation of the Hannah Stanley Opportunity School, the name "Haywood" was no longer a part of Anna's life. Focusing on adults unable to attend school during the day, the Stanley School was open evenings to serve Black women still forced to spend their days as household servants.[7]

More than either of her siblings, Anna Cooper was a child of freedom. Born just a few years before President Abraham Lincoln's official declaration of war on the South, she had learned to walk and talk within a traumatic and shifting environment. Life in North Carolina, and especially in the capital city of Raleigh, would have guaranteed exposure to chaotic and frightening events. When the army of North Carolina finally surrendered to W.T. Sherman on April 26, 1865, few outside of the Black community could imagine that an equally significant gathering of darker citizens would occur just months later. Nonetheless, by the Fourth of July, 2,000 former slaves celebrated their freedom by parading through the main streets of the capital city. The march, ending at the governor's house, was followed by a series of Black town meetings held throughout the state. Along with church gatherings, such meetings culminated in a State Convention of Colored

Citizens. This was evidence that newly freed men and women were developing their own internal social and political structures. Even a young witness to those events such as Anna Cooper would have understood that something of significance was taking place.

It was, however, the opening of schoolhouses that would have made a more direct impression on the young. Described by one newspaper as having a "disease for learning," Black North Carolinians saw reading and writing as proof of freedom for themselves and their children. Located in Raleigh, St. Augustine Normal School was among the hundreds of institutions that had opened their doors by 1868. In January of that year, children who had only known slavery were gathered into spaces more recently used as barracks for Confederate soldiers. One of those students, Anna Cooper, later remembered it as a time when "our girls as well as our boys flocked in and battled for an education."[8]

The years at St. Augustine were formative in both academic and personal ways for "Annie," as she was then known. It was not long before the student became a teacher, as "little Annie" was put to work teaching to others lessons she had recently mastered. Her life as an educator began when she was so young and small that a chair was needed in order that she might be seen and heard. Given the opportunity to function in the roles of both student and teacher also presented Cooper with the first of many obstacles in completing her own education. After having to cajole her way into a course open to male students only, Anna's anger at having to do so was stored away and recalled with irritation decades later.[9] After completing the requirements for a high school diploma, Anna graduated from St. Augustine and married an instructor, George A.C. Cooper, a native of the Bahamas. Two years after their marriage, George became an ordained Episcopal Priest, but within months he died of what Anna described as "hard work and exposure while serving his parish." Now a widow at the age of 21, Anna Cooper focused on her teaching job and taking more courses at St. Augustine. It would not be long before her "thumping from within" sent her in search of more advanced course work.[10]

Oberlin College was the most logical next step, so Anna made her way to Ohio. Founded in 1833, Oberlin College holds the distinction of being the first coeducational college in the U.S., as well as the first to welcome African American students. With decidedly abolitionist leanings, the college had already admitted more than 100 Black students, both male and female, before the Civil War. This population included both ex-slaves and freeborn Blacks.[11] In choosing Oberlin, Cooper followed in the footsteps of Mar'gru Sarah Kinson, as well as Mary Jane Patterson, another North Carolina native. Patterson went on to become the first African American woman to receive a four-year degree from a U.S. college. Although admittedly not the "superior northern college" Anna had originally hoped for, Oberlin proved an excellent fit for Cooper's inquisitive mind. The promise of a scholarship, in addition to assisting with housing and summer employment, paved the way for the near-destitute young woman.

Unhampered by either spoken or unspoken disapproval of female intrusion into courses meant for males, Anna Cooper immersed herself in classes in mathematics and ancient languages. Completing her studies in 1884, Anna graduated along with two other Black women, Mary Eliza Church and Ida A. Gibbs. Anna was the only one of the trio who had been born into slavery and was solely responsible for securing her own education. The most affluent of the group, Mary Church, had come to Oberlin from the Black elite of Memphis, Tennessee. Her parents not only paid for her education, but also sent her on a long extended stay in "some of the principal cities in England, Belgium, Switzerland, and France."[12] While not as well off as Mary Church, Ida Gibbs also came from an exceptional and exceptionally well-educated background.

Her father, Mifflin Wistar Gibbs, was an entrepreneur and somewhat of a traveling political activist. Mifflin had run for office and become involved in race issues in such disparate places as California, Arkansas, and British Columbia. In 1897, President William McKinley appointed Gibbs the U.S. Consul for the island of Madagascar. While less is known of Ida's mother, Maria Alexander Gibbs, there can be little doubt that she played a significant part in the education of her children. During the 1860s, Alexander's own family had sent her alone from Kentucky to Ohio in order to attend Oberlin. There can be little doubt that when she returned to Oberlin as a wife and mother in 1870, she did so in pursuit of education for her own children.[13] In the company of such privileged Black women, Anna Cooper was an unmistakable outsider. The trio had many shared experiences during and after college, but Mary Church and Ida Gibbs never managed a close relationship with Cooper.[14] However, some 70 years later, it was at Cooper's home that they gathered to reminisce about their days at Oberlin.[15]

After graduation, Anna Cooper found work as an itinerant educator. At first, teaching Latin and mathematics, she moved on to serve a short stint as head of the Department of Modern Language and Science at Wilberforce University. That was followed by a return home to North Carolina to teach math, Latin and Greek at her alma mater, St. Augustine's. In 1887, Cooper received a call that would have excited any African American educator of the era. Offered a position at the Preparatory School for Colored Youth in Washington, D.C., she relocated to the city that would become her home until her death.[16]

To live in the nation's capital at the turn of the century was to be immersed in a place of special significance to Black Americans. In search of safety and work at the end of the Civil War, scores of newly freed and destitute African Americans had made their way to the city. The presence of

Howard University, chartered in 1867, provided a community for the Black intelligentsia. Migrants in the area included political and social leaders such as Frederick Douglass, Blanch K. Bruce and P.B.S. Pinchback. Thus, long before Cooper's arrival, the District of Columbia had become home to the Black masses, along with a smaller middle class and an even smaller (but definitely visible) Black social elite. The size of the population, combined with many whites' reluctance to serve them as customers, opened the door to Black entrepreneurship. This led to the growth of African American business owners, including undertakers, life insurance providers, photographers and building and loan societies. One such—The Industrial Building and Savings Company—was the forerunner of the first Black-owned bank in the country. By the turn of the century, there were close to 300 Black businesses in the District of Columbia, as well as several news publications and numerous churches of every denomination.[17]

Not even D.C.'s dynamic setting appears to have intimidated the ever-confident Anna Cooper. Her intelligence, growing public visibility and unflinching personality were a perfect fit for Washington, D.C.;[18] at least Cooper thought so, and she was ready to "build a home, not merely a house to shelter the body, but a home to sustain and refresh the mind ... where friends foregather for interchange of ideas and agreeable association of sympathetic spirits." She lived and worked in the nation's capital but also "planted my little North Carolina Colony" as well.[19] In this setting, Cooper slowly began a trek toward her greatest accomplishments.

By the last decade of the 1800s, Anna had laid the foundation for the life that would take her into the middle of the twentieth century. It was a time of great discovery, and one in which it might be said that she was also discovered. A much-loved job teaching high school math and science was the center of her world, but during these years Cooper also increasingly moved onto the public stage as a respected intellectual. Black Americans, particularly women, were never far from the center of Cooper's discourse in any medium. In both print and public addresses, she raised uncomfortable and sometimes challenging concerns. No institution or segment of society was above her scrutiny. In a speech before a convention of Black Episcopal Churchmen, she reminded some and educated others by pointing out that Church history provided evidence of a "double offense against woman ... Making of marriage a sacrament and at the same time insisting on the celibacy of the clergy ... to reflect discredit on woman. Would this were all or the worst! But the Church by the Licentiousness of its chosen servants invaded the household and established ... relations which it forbade."[20]

In 1892, Cooper was equally direct when she spoke before the Congress of Representative Women at the Chicago World's Fair. White women, who fought to be included in organizing programs for the event, had not themselves included Blacks. When Black women protested, an exception was made, allowing Anna Cooper and Fannie Barrier Williams to give speeches. Before reminding the audience of the progress that African Americans had made, Cooper spoke of "the darkest period of the colored women's oppression in this country," and the "silent toil of mothers to gain ... title to the bodies of their daughters .... The white woman could at least plead for her own emancipation, the black woman, double enslaved, could but suffer and struggle and be silent." She informed her overwhelmingly white audience that "we take our stand on the solidarity of humanity...and the unnaturalness and injustice of all special favoritisms, whether of sex, race, country, or condition."[21]

Cooper's ideas were no less fearless and provocative in print. Also published in 1892, her book, *A Voice From the South by a Black Woman of the South*, was well received by Black and white reviewers alike and exposed her to a wider audience.[22]

Described over a century later as an early Black feminist treatise, her collection of essays is balanced on interlocking issues of race, gender, class, and politics. Considering no subject beyond her reach, Cooper took direct, fearless and unflattering aim at the white South.

> "One of the ... facts about the unwritten history of this country is the ... ability with which Southern influence, ... ideas and ... ideals, have from the very beginning even up to the present day, dictated to and dominated over ... this nation. Without wealth, without education, without inventions, arts, sciences, or industries, without ... any of the progressive ideas ... which have made this country great .... Personally indolent and practically stupid, poor in everything but bluster and self-esteem, the Southerner has nevertheless ... succeeded ... in shaping the policy of this government to suit his purposes. Indeed the Southerner is a magnificent manager of men."[23]

Focusing her critical attention directly on white women, Cooper observed, "Now the Southern woman, I may be pardoned, being one myself, was never renowned for her reasoning powers, and it is not surprising that just a little picking will make her logic fall." A Black contemporary of Cooper's, Gertrude Bustill Mossell, pronounced the book "one of the finest contributions yet made toward the solution of the Negro problem."[24]

Anna Cooper's involvement in public life included founding as well as joining a number of organizations intent on addressing issues affecting "the race." She became a charter member of Washington, D.C.'s Colored Women's League, co-founded the Washington Negro Folklore Society and worked with the District of Columbia's "alley sanitation" committee. The focus of the committee was to address the daily concerns of homeless families forced to live in the alleyways of the nation's capital.

As an independent working woman with economic responsibility for herself and other family members, she had to conduct community activism in tandem with teaching and other duties at the M Street School. None of these responsibilities, however, prevented Anna from thinking beyond the borders of her own country. In 1891, through her work as an educator, Cooper took advantage of the opportunity to experience another country and culture. While participating in a cultural exchange program with Black teachers in Canada, Anna penned a letter home to her "dear mother." Writing to one whose movements had been strictly controlled by law and brutal force, Cooper carefully described the freedom and openness of the streets and the people in the city of Toronto. Within the next decade, Anna Cooper would cast her sights farther and farther away from America. Taking place in 1896, her next venture was more personal than professional. Cooper traveled to the West Indies on a visit to Nassau, the place of her husband's birth.[25] By 1900, not at all daunted by the prospects of crossing the mighty Atlantic Ocean, Cooper boarded a steamship for her first transatlantic voyage.

Along with three other Black American women, Cooper had been invited to attend an international gathering of people of African descent. Taking place in London at Westminster Town Hall, the primary aim of the meeting was to discuss political and economic issues encountered by Blacks around the world. This small precursor to what would become known as the Pan-African Movement included representatives of African descent from Ethiopia, Haiti, Liberia, Sierra Leone, Ghana and the Caribbean. Delegates and attendees from the United States included Bishop Alexander Walters and W. E. B. Du Bois. A small number of women in attendance were active participants, with both Cooper and Anna Jones of Missouri delivering papers. Alongside Du Bois, Anna was elected to serve on the executive committee. Among their responsibilities was drafting a formal statement protesting the treatment of African peoples around the globe. Their statement was the first coming from outside of Africa to protest the treatment of Blacks in South Africa to be forwarded to Queen Victoria. Although probably unexpected, a response was received some five months later. Members of the committee were assured of Her Majesty's concern for the "interest and welfare" of her kingdom's "native races."[26] Along with the male members of the conference, Anna Cooper and the other women had actively involved themselves in the gathering that is said to have put the word "Pan-African" in the dictionary for the first time.[27]

Leaving London, Anna Cooper joined other Black Americans to attend the World's Fair in Paris. Formally known as the *Exposition Universelle*, the Fair included more than 100 nations and drew 50,000,000 visitors during seven months of operation. With the theme of welcoming the new century, the Fair focused on recent inventions, ideas and products. Fully operational models of moving escalators, talking film, panoramic paintings and the largest refracting telescope of the time were presented as pathways into the next century. Given Anna Cooper's love of math and science, the focus of the Fair alone would have captured her attention; that the event also included an *"Expose' ne'gre"* (Negro Exposition) assured her interest. The exhibit was proudly presented as "planned and executed by Negroes." Organized with the help of W. E. B. Du Bois and Thomas J. Calloway, the project included near-life-sized depictions of various Black communities. Census data and information from the Library of Congress were supplemented with hundreds of photographs of neatly dressed Black men, women and children. In keeping with the Fair's theme of progress, displays were designed to inform the world of the extraordinary accomplishments of Blacks in America. In less than 40 years after the end of slavery, 60 percent of Black children were attending school; newly freed people had written for more than 1,400 publications and registered 350 patents.[28] It is hard to imagine that Cooper did not link the path that her own life had taken to the charts and pictures in the exhibit. Although born a slave, she had managed to travel across the Atlantic Ocean to participate in events that mattered to her. Unlike her associate, Du Bois, she had been offered no stipend to offset the expenses of her first voyage outside of the continental United States. She had nonetheless found the means to finance this and would do the same for future travels.[29]

None of the progress and new inventions presented at the World's Fair could, nor did, dramatically affect the lives of the visiting Black Americans. Cooper and her fellow travelers returned home to continue their lives as usual. After being promoted to the position of principal at M Street High School in 1902, Anna continued her efforts to prepare Black students for entry into the best colleges in America. After revising the curriculum, the next step was replacing the textbooks that had been mandated by an all-white governing board. Declaring the books "racially derogatory," Anna continued headlong with her own efforts. She not only secured written agreements from several prestigious colleges assuring her that qualified students would be admitted, Cooper also led a search to acquire funding for scholarships.[30] Inevitably, the whirlwind of potential change collided with the internal and external politics of the schools, and the proposed new directions generated formidable foes. Her new strategies were in direct opposition to the leading Black voice in America, Booker T. Washington. Even as Washington and his infamous "Tuskegee Machine" confirmed manual and industrial education as the model for Black education, Cooper was fighting to strengthen college preparatory courses. While maintaining vocational programs at M Street School, she strongly objected to any educational philosophies that put a ceiling on educational opportunities for African Americans.[31]

As public and acrimonious debate on the subject of Black education continued between the leading "race men" of the day, Booker T. Washington and W. E. B. Du Bois, Anna Cooper invited Du Bois to speak at M Street school. Giving a presentation strongly supportive of Cooper's philosophy, Du Bois fiercely criticized whites who assumed Blacks were incapable of the same intellectual pursuits as themselves. With the backing of an all-white school board, Principal Cooper soon found herself charged by the school board with insubordination and "running the school at her own discretion."[32]

Not even accolades received from a notable foreign visitor could forestall the inevitable. On an official tour to study schools and churches in the United States and Canada, Abbé Felix Klein, a professor from the Catholic Institute of Paris, arrived in Washington D.C., in 1905. Sanctioned with a letter from the president of the Board of Education, Klein inspected every school in the nation's capital. Following his unannounced arrival at the "colored" school, Principle Cooper treated Klein to a guided tour of the premises. Klein would later write of that experience: "To see these 530 young negroes and negresses ... under teachers of their own race, pursuing the same studies as our average college students, who would dream of the existence of a terrible race question in the United States?"[33]

In spite of such observations, outrageous rumors began to surface, slandering Cooper's personal and professional reputation. Charges of "inefficiency and inability to maintain good decorum" at the school were coupled with suggestions of romantic links to a younger man. By the time that official charges were completed, allegations had become vague accusations of inappropriate "sympathetic teaching methods." In an act of incomprehensible ire, a school board subcommittee settled on a broad spectrum of transgressions, including that of helping "unqualified and weak students...and not maintaining loyalty to the director of high schools." It was agreed that Anna Cooper would not be removed from her position providing that "in her official role she shall recognize the authority of ... the director of high schools, and conform her official conduct in all respect to rules of the board."[34]

The verdict was but a temporary reprieve, as the governing board subsequently voted not to rehire Cooper. The unrepentant and unemployed school principal responded with her own demands for reinstatement of her job and back salary. Aware that she would receive neither, Cooper secured another position at the Lincoln Institute in Missouri. Her job now included serving as the chair of languages and teaching courses in Latin and Greek. Of her recent ordeal, she would write with both jauntiness and keen political awareness, "The dominant forces of our country are not yet tolerant of the higher steps for colored youth ... so ... my head was lost in the fray and I moved west ... But if the industrializing wave that threatens, reaches us here too, it is likely to be another case of 'Move along, Joe!'"[35]

Called back to Washington, D.C., by a new school administration after four years of what Cooper referred to as her "exile," Anna returned to M Street High School in 1910. This time she accepted a position as a Latin teacher, an assignment that remained hers for the next two decades. This apparently preferred return to full-time instruction marked the beginning of a new phase of life.

A shift in focus to her own education would send Cooper once again to distant shores. Encouraged by conversations of five years earlier with the Frenchman Felix Klein, Anna Cooper spent the summers of 1911 through 1913 taking courses at *La Guilde Internationale* in Paris.[36] Acquiring certificates in French literature, history and phonetics seemed to whet her appetite for more. By 1914, a long and circuitous trek toward a Ph.D. began to take shape with courses at Columbia University. What would have been an arduous undertaking for any woman during the early twentieth century required supreme confidence and exceptionally good fortune for one who had been born a slave.

In spite of her movement both within the country and abroad, North Carolina and her extended family always occupied a central place in Anna Cooper's life. Within that framework, at the age of 55, Anna became the surrogate mother and sole provider for five great-nieces and nephews: Regia, John, Andrew, Marion and Annie, all of whom were under 12 years of age. The youngest, Annie Cooper, named after her great aunt, was approximately six months old. The circumstances that required instant transformation in the life of the aging schoolteacher were tragic but not uncommon among African Americans of the era. Recalling the details long after her great-nieces and nephews had reached adulthood, Anna wrote: "At Dawn on Christmas Day, in 1915 I walked into the … cottage in Raleigh where lay five sleeping children whose mother had lately been called to Heaven. Not all were asleep, the baby of six months was awake … immediately began to coo … and held out both arms as if she knew something was happening."

On more than one occasion, Anna's household had expanded to include younger relatives and friends;[37] however, being faced with a "little North Carolina colony" of children introduced a variety of new hurdles. In a rare move for Black Americans, the children were all legally adopted and the new mother was *"at some pains to find a place in Washington that would be a home to house their Southern exuberance."* The problem was solved with $10.00 and a contract to purchase a house. Although the building had previously been "used as a chicken yard," there was room enough to accommodate the large family.[38] For a single woman who had always worked for her daily bread, there could have been few illusions concerning these newly acquired burdens. Cooper had now joined the ranks of other single parents in attempting to stretch both wages and time to new limits. Her own writings suggest that she approached mothering with a critical eye. Years earlier, she had described an infant as "a constant drain on the capital of its parents ... it is to be fed, and worked for, and sheltered and protected .... it is a parasite, a thief." Mothers were depicted as "infatuated" beings that would not sell a child for its "weight in gold." Writing with both a cynical and comedic eye, Anna Cooper concluded that "[n]o one will ever tempt her [a mother] with any such offer. The world knows ... well what an outlay of time and money and labor must be made before he is worth even his weight in ashes."[39]

Given such blunt observations, one might wonder just what forces pulled or pushed Cooper to assume such responsibility. Her response, though, was in complete alignment with her overall philosophy; they were simply and unsentimentally her family. They were taken "under my wing with the hope and determination of nurturing their growth into useful and creditable citizenship."[40] Whatever her original motivation, Cooper was a surrogate mother to the three girls and two boys for the rest of her life. To her credit and their own, by the mid-1920s Regia was attending St. Augustine college and John was at Tuskegee, while Andrew and Marion were at schools in Virginia. Her namesake, little Annie, graduated from Dunbar and attended school in Virginia. When Cooper died years later, a newspaper article listed "two great nieces and a nephew," all at her address.[41]

Entanglements of family life and work presented obstacles and detours, but not an end to Cooper's own plans to earn a Ph.D.[42] When the youngest child reached school age, Cooper began to ease her own education back onto the center stage of her life. Unable to see the road ahead clearly, she stubbornly plodded onward with what was referred to as "homework" for Columbia University. In addition to ongoing battles to keep her job at M Street School, there was difficulty in completing Columbia's one-year residency requirement. The impossibility of meeting such a condition was not a deterrent but a call to look in other directions. In the summer of 1924, with the encouragement of her old friend Felix Klein, Cooper returned to France. She did so this time as a doctoral student at the Sorbonne in Paris. Summers at a university in France could be managed when a year's residency at Columbia could not. A transfer of credits from Columbia University coupled with a fellowship from the Alpha Kappa Alpha sorority made it possible for Cooper to continue the determined march toward her degree. By the spring of 1925, the seemingly impossible battle was all but won. The occasion recorded in her memoir is simply remembered as "with my typed MS in my handbag I once again crossed the Atlantic." The manuscript that was held so closely was her dissertation, which Cooper was returning to the Sorbonne to defend, in French. Having done so successfully, Anna Julia Cooper boarded yet another ship to retrace her steps back to the United States.[43]

Anna J. Cooper's degree was formally awarded on December 29, 1925, in "a pleasing ceremony" at Howard University in Washington, D.C. Under the auspices of her sorority Alpha Kappa Alpha, at 66 years of age Cooper was ushered into a rare circle. Not only had she become the fourth African American woman to earn a doctorate, but she was also the first Black woman to earn a Ph.D. from the Sorbonne.[44]

Having reached the goal she had been working toward for so much of her life was no indication that it was time to retire from the public eye. Leaving M Street School (now renamed Dunbar High School) at the age of 70, Cooper immediately took over the helm of financially strapped Frelinghuysen University.[45] Never a college in the traditional sense, Frelinghuysen was more a collection of educational and social programs meeting in separate locations around the city. Founded in the early 1900s in response to a broad spectrum of needs in the African American community, the project had already survived several incarnations. The one consistent thread was a commitment to the education of the Black masses. The philosophy embraced learners "untouched" by any schoolhouse in the past, as well as those whose daytime employment made attendance at Howard University impossible.

In accepting the presidency of Frelinghuysen on June 15, 1930, Anna Cooper embarked on her last official position as an educator. Her new challenge was to stabilize an institution committed to educating "those furthest down the economic ladder and with the greatest need." With her political tongue still sharp, Cooper created her own special project for those "intentionally left out." The program, the Hannah Stanley School, was dedicated "in the name of my slave Mother to the education of colored working people," and Cooper would later describe it as superseding her doctorate in importance.[46] Almost as destitute as the population making its way through the doors, by 1940 the floundering Frelinguysen University simply moved into Cooper's own large house. Now in her 80s, Anna relinquished the presidency but continued to work with and for the school until 1949.[47]

In the years that followed, the lack of a formal attachment to any educational institution did not seem to relieve the aging educator of her opinions. At the age of 100, Anna Cooper did not mince words when a newspaper reporter asked for her thoughts on *Brown v. Board of Education*. As others celebrated the Supreme Court decision finding segregation illegal, Anna Cooper pronounced that she was against it. Desegregation, she predicted, would be the end of "race conscience education." With the experience of more than 70 years at various levels of education, Cooper did not believe that the country had progressed to the point that it would "teach black children .... to take pride in themselves and their heritage." Seemingly out of step with the undoubtedly political breakthrough of her time, and too easily chalked up to advanced age, Cooper had once again dared to trouble the waters.[48]

Chapter 3

On February 27, 1964, approaching 106 years of age, Anna Cooper died peacefully at her home in Washington, D.C. She had stated her desires clearly in a will, leaving her beloved home to the Frelinghuysen School with the simple declaration: "I cannot take it with me."[49] On March. 4th, funeral services were held in the chapel of St. Augustine College in Raleigh, North Carolina. "Little Annie," who had stood on a chair to teach her first students, had lived to affect the lives of untold others. Propelled by her own "innate wanting to know," she had moved away from St. Augustine, mastered modern and foreign languages, earned degrees in mathematics and French history, and crossed the Atlantic Ocean more than once before returning to the first place she had called home. Following the funeral services, Dr. Anna Julia Cooper was buried in the Hargett Street Cemetery in Raleigh. She lies at rest next to George A.C. Cooper, the husband of her youth. In time, her life and work would be remembered by both church and state. In the first instance, the Liturgical calendar of the Episcopal Church (USA) has recognized her work as an educator by earmarking February 28 as Anna Julia Cooper Feast day. At the other end of the spectrum, more than four decades after her death, Cooper would be remembered by her country with her words stamped into the United States Passport "The cause of freedom is not the cause of a race or a sect, a party or a class—it is the cause of humankind, the very birthright of humanity."

Chapter Four

Mary Church Terrell: Daughter of Privilege, Activist by Choice

Anna J. Cooper and Mary Church both belonged to a cluster of African Americans born into a world transitioning from slavery to the Emancipation Proclamation. Cooper, born between 1858 and 1860 in North Carolina, and Terrell, born in 1863 in Tennessee, were both residents of states in which actual Civil War battles took place. Men, women and children, Black and white across the Confederate states, suffered greatly, but those caught in the crosshairs of combat were especially vulnerable. Anna Cooper and Mary Church shared the trauma of that experience, but it is their differences that broaden our understanding of nineteenth century Black women's lives and movements at home and abroad.

Mary Eliza Church, or "Mollie" as she was called, was born into a family of newly freed slaves who succeeded beyond all expectations. She belonged to a small community that emerged at the top of the African-American class structure in the decades immediately following the Civil War. Many within this elite group were clearly of mixed bloodlines. Theirs was a world in which varying degrees of benefits might be wrung. An equal or larger number of those wearing the badge of race mixing experienced poverty, scorn and trauma. Whenever humanly possible, those who were able did everything to shield themselves and their families from some of the daily insults and violence endured by the masses of freed African-Americans. None, however, were free of the stigma of supposed racial inferiority. Given her membership with such a group, it might be supposed that Mary Church Terrell's life trajectory would resemble that of a privileged white woman of her era. This was, however, not the case. Before her death in 1954 at more than 90 years of age, she had lived her life in a way unimaginable to most self-possessed, indulged women of means. Working through various stages of racial accommodation and resistance, she eventually evolved into a formidable fighter in the battle for civil rights and social reform. Mary Church knew, entertained, corresponded with and disagreed with political and social movers and shakers of her day. Her acquaintances included Booker T. Washington, Susan B. Anthony, Paul Lawrence Dunbar, W. E. B. Du Bois, H. G. Wells, and Ida B. Wells Barnett. Clearly, many aspects of Mary Church Terrell's life bore little resemblance to those lived by the vast majority of Black women of her time. That included earning a college degree, traveling abroad, and marrying a *cum laude* graduate of Harvard University.[1] None of these "benefits" proved to be safeguards against the lethal mob violence that was visited upon her circle of family and friends. Unrestrained brutality and disrespect witnessed in her early years formed the bedrock of Mary Church Terrell's push for civil rights and social reform.

Born on September 23, 1863 in Memphis, Tennessee, Mary Eliza Church came into the world poised between the end of slavery and the ambiguity of freedom. While the recently passed Emancipation Proclamation freed all slaves in states under Confederate control, those in the Union-held Tennessee were technically still not free; nonetheless, Memphis and the surrounding areas became a haven for both freed and runaway slaves defined by military language as "contraband of war." The infant Mollie had been born of slave parents, Robert Reed Church and Louisa Ayers. Both of mixed-race parentage, Robert and Louisa had slave mothers and slave-owning fathers.

Robert Church was the son and slave of Captain Charles B. Church, a Mississippi riverboat captain. Working aboard his father's vessels as a boy, Robert gained invaluable skills, but never received a formal education. He taught himself to read and write, "but he never wrote a letter in his life." Ties between the two men were apparently durable enough to at least acknowledge the next generation. As a very small child, Mollie took Sunday excursions with her father by buggy "to see Captain C.B. Church," a man who looked like her father. When questioned about the similarity between the men, an explanation was given "in a very matter of fact natural sort of way." While it is clear that Mary believed her father had been a slave and the "Captain" was her grandfather, subsequent generations of the Church clan have tended to focus on the pleasant working relationship between the father and son.[2]

Mary's maternal lineage provided her with a different story, but one not dissimilar from her father's. Louisa Ayers also had been a slave, but she "never referred to that fact." When pushed for more information, Louisa offered stories of a master whose family had taught her to read and write and had given her lessons in French. In fact, when Louisa married Robert Church, she had been given a "wedding trousseau bought in New York" by her master's daughter. Guests at the ceremony were treated to "a delicious repast." But that delightful bit of history did not tell the whole story. Louisa Ayers's own mother, Eliza, provides a different perspective. The "very dark, almost black" slave woman had been a "housekeeper to ole miss" and when she gave birth, the child, Louisa, was taken away from her. Apparently kept somewhere in her owner's family, the child was eventually reunited with her mother either just before or during the Civil War.

In addition to bearing her "very dark" grandmother's name, Mary Eliza Church had regular exposure to, and great affection for, the woman who had lived most of her own life as a slave. She was entertained for hours by "Gramma Eliza's" words, some of which left an impression readily recalled nearly a half-century later. As an adult, Mary Church Terrell had not forgotten the tales of "brutality perpetrated upon slaves who belong to cruel masters." She also remembered her grandmother's tearful reassurance, "Never mind honey ... Gramma ain't a slave no more."[3] Even in her own comfortable freedom, Terrell came to her understanding of slavery and race and their effects on women through a very personal lens. Well into the twentieth century, she penned in her autobiography,

> When slavery is discussed and somebody rhapsodizes upon the goodness and kindness of masters and mistresses toward their slaves ..., it is hard for me to conceal my disgust. There is no doubt that some slaveholders were kind to their slaves. Captain Church was one of them, and this daughter of a slave father is glad ... publicly to express her gratitude ... but the anguish of one slave mother from whom her baby was snatched away outweighs all the kindness and goodness which were occasionally shown a fortunate, favored slave.

Mary Church Terrell had even more intimate reasons to question the inner lives of Black women, whether they were among the "favored" or not. It is never more clearly stated than in the opening sentences of her autobiography. She introduces her birth with something akin to gallows humor:

> TO TELL THE TRUTH, I came very near not being on this mundane sphere at all. In a fit of despondency my dear mother tried to end her life a few months before I was born. By a miracle she was saved, and I finally arrived on scheduled time none the worse for the prenatal experience which might have proved decidedly disagreeable, if not fatal, to my future.

Although describing her mother as a constant "ray of sunshine" with "an infectious laugh," Mary also recognized her as a woman with "troubles of her own, financial, domestic and otherwise."[4] We are left to speculate what propelled a woman of her social standing to unwrap such private matters for public consumption. Published in 1940, Mary Church Terrell's autobiography came into print in an era when potential readers—Black or white—would have considered such details better left undisclosed. It was, in fact, evidence of an unconventional side of Terrell's life and personality. Although close to her parents throughout their lives, Robert and Louisa were, in their daughter's eyes, "as different as one human being can be from another." Confiding in an unpublished essay, Mary wrote, "Constant quarreling in the home embitters the life of a child…causing him to despise one or the other of his parent." In the Terrell household, differences ultimately led to divorce when Mary and her brother were quite young.[5]

Long before she was one of the leading luminaries within the privileged circle of Black Washington, D.C., Mary Eliza Church was the daughter of a Memphis saloonkeeper whose wife dressed the hair of wealthy white women. While her father would eventually become labeled "the wealthiest colored man in Tennessee, and the richest black man in the South," Mollie Church described her mother's role as something beyond that of the simple, traditionally defined "helpmate." It was Louisa Church's success as the owner of a hair salon that paid for "the first home and the first carriage we had." Robert Church eventually provided both his first and second families with luxuries beyond the means of most Americans of any race, but in his early years, his wife ensured the family's financial stability.[6]

Although more financially independent than most newly freed Blacks, the Church family was also irrevocably linked to the Memphis Black community. The reality of their position was brought into sharp focus in an incident that nearly cost

Robert Church his life. It also exposed his young daughter to the fact of unrestrained public violence against Blacks, no matter their station in life. In the years immediately following the Civil War, the environment in Memphis and other cities that had been occupied by federal troops was rife with hostility towards Black citizens. For many white citizens, difficulties in rebuilding their lives had been exacerbated by the presence of Northerners as well as the increase in the number of Blacks, including some still in uniform. The Freedmen's Bureau, along with an Irish population almost as impoverished as Blacks, added another ingredient to the pot. In early May 1866, everything came to a boil, spilling over into the streets. In what is referred to as the "Memphis Massacre," or alternatively, the "Irish or Nigger Riots," the city was taken over by roaming white mobs bent on the destruction of Black life and property. While attempting to protect his business from the rioters, Robert Church became a victim when he was shot in the head. Although Mollie was only three at the time, the event had a lasting effect on the entire family. Her father's "violent temper" was attributed to the bullet that left "a hole in the back of his head ... into which one could insert the tip of the little finger." Robert Church was never rid of "headaches so severe he wanted to kill himself." Terrell believed that her father actually would have been killed "if the rioters had not believed they had finished him off when he fell to the ground."[7]

The riot finally was quelled when federal troops placed the city under martial law. The true gravity and rampant spread of violence were described clearly in a congressional committee report:

> The proportions of what is called the "riot," but in reality the massacre, proved to be far more extended, and the circumstances surrounding it of much greater significance, than the committee had any conception

of ... The mob finding itself under the protection and guidance of official authority, and sustained by ... powerful public ... feelings of the most deadly hatred to the colored race, ... proceeded with deliberation to the commission of .... horrors which can scarcely find a parallel in the history of civilized or barbarous nations, and must inspire the profound emotions of horror among all civilized people. ... The whole evidence discloses the killing of men, women, and children—the innocent, unarmed and defenseless pleading for their lives and crying for mercy; the wounding, beating, and maltreating of a still greater number; burning, pillaging, and robbing; the consuming of dead bodies in the flames, the burning of dwellings, the attempts to burn up whole families in their houses, and the brutal and revolting ravishing of defenseless and terror-stricken women.[8]

While one tragedy nearly cost Robert Church his life, a second disaster a dozen years later helped him build an economic foundation for succeeding generations. When one of a series of Yellow Fever epidemics struck the city of Memphis in 1879, Robert Church hurried his visiting children back to their mother in New York. Escorting them by train as far as Cincinnati, Ohio, he returned to Memphis to begin what some considered a daring if not foolish venture. Even as it was being declared a doomed city, Robert Church believed that Memphis and its people could be salvaged. By strategically purchasing land and claiming abandoned properties, he was prepared when the city recovered. Within a few years, Church was wealthy enough to build a hotel, as well as the country's largest meeting and entertainment center for Blacks. In 1899, he erected an amusement park on Beale Street, and a few years later, Robert became the founding president of the Solvent Savings Bank and Trust Company. The presence of this first Black bank in the city was cause for undeniable pride, but in a city that allowed Black citizens no access to "public" recreational facilities, the amusement park reached a broader segment of the marginalized population.

In recounting her own brush with yellow fever, Mary Church wrote with undeniable pride in her father, "a recently emancipated slave who had never gone to school a day in his life," who had nonetheless "outsmarted ... many men who had graduated from college, and who had great reputations for keen business acumen."

Not only was he a man of business—or perhaps because he was a businessman—Robert Church also delved into politics in his city. As African Americans pushed for citizenship rights in the years following emancipation and reconstruction, Church was one of the men daring enough to run for public office. Losing his first attempt as a candidate for the Board of Public Works in 1882, he eventually accrued enough political muscle to be elected to serve as a delegate to the Republican National Convention of 1900.[9]

While Mary Church Terrell's early life was shaped by the unusual degree of security and comfort provided by both of her parents, she was also affected by the troubled relationship between the two. That she learned to navigate her way through a tangled web of family ties may have prepared her for roles she would play later in life. She was clearly attached to, and proud of, her father who was not just a talented businessman. He loved to cook special dishes for his daughter and willingly risked the ire of a teacher by interrupting the school day to bring his child a toy. But earning the undying love of his offspring did not spare him her judicious adult observations. Mary Church was well aware that her father "had the vices and defects common to men born at that time." In spite of the pain and embarrassment caused by her parents' separation and subsequent divorce before she was sixteen, Mary did not fix blame. Looking back on the matter, she noted, "In those days divorces were not so common as they are now, and no matter what caused the separation of a couple, the woman was usually blamed." In the end, her father could not be painted a "saint" and her mother had lifelong "troubles of her own."[10]

Whatever caused the couple to go their separate ways, they both remained an active presence in the lives of both their children. By 1879 and the Yellow Fever episode, Louisa Ayers had already sold her hair salon in Memphis and was living in New York. Opening another hair salon on Sixth Avenue in New York helped provide a comfortable living for the family. Remaining in Memphis, Robert Church also seemed to have added willingly and substantially toward that end. With his help, Mollie was sent to Ohio to attend Oberlin High School and then Oberlin College. Even as her parents resided in different states and she in a third, Mary Church could still depend on her mother to send her "beautiful clothes from New York bought with the money that Father had sent her for that purpose."[11] Graduating college in 1884 placed Mary among the few women of her race to have done so just two decades after the Civil War. That she and two other black women (Anna J. Cooper and Ida Gibbs) had each earned bachelors degrees from Oberlin's rigorous "gentlemen's course" was a matter of individual, race and gender pride.[12] Having generously supported their daughter's education, for some unexplained reason, neither Robert nor Louisa attended her graduation. Each parent recognized Mary's accomplishment in his and her own way. From her mother, Mary received "a wonderful black jet dress, for the young women who graduated from the 'gentlemen's course' always dressed in somber black ... She also sent me a pair of opera glasses ... it did not compensate me for her absence."

Having transformed himself into a "gentleman" of more than ample means, Robert Church's gift to Mary for her graduation called attention to that fact. Telling his daughter to meet him in Louisville, Kentucky, for a "nice visit," he also informed her that she would be returning to Tennessee to live in his home in Memphis. Now 21 years of age, Mary found the stay in her father's newly erected 14-room Queen Anne-style home both comfortable and short-lived. Within a year Robert Church announced his intention to remarry, relieving his daughter of her duties as the official hostess of the Church household.[13] An increasing sense of idleness and displacement set her on a path that would earn her the label of "Genteel Militant." Fully aware that her father's belief in the conventions of middle-class southern society would not permit her to "actively engage in any work outside of the home," Mary Church moved to New York for a "visit" with her mother. From that post she began to pursue what had become a nagging desire to put her education to good use. Ignoring her father's admonition that she would be "taking the bread and butter out of the mouth of some girl who needed it," she began to search for a position at "one of the colored schools."[14] Given the dearth of Black women with college degrees, she quickly found employment at Wilberforce College in Ohio.

Occupying one of the most prestigious and lucrative forms of employment that a Black workingwoman could have brought an end to any sense of idleness. This high-status position came with a heavy and broadly defined workload. Given the responsibility for teaching "five classes in subjects totally dissimilar," including college-level French and mineralogy, Mary was also expected to instruct basic reading and writing in the preparatory college. The position also required service as the "secretary of the faculty" and church organist for two services every Sunday, as well as directing choir during the week. For fulfilling this wide-ranging but typical set of duties, Mollie Church was paid "the munificent salary of $40.00 per month." Exhilarated at having earned her own money and even managing to save "the fabulously large sum" of $150.00, there was only one disappointment in her life: her father had cut off all communication. After an initial letter filled with outrage at his daughter's "disobedience," Robert Church severed all connections. He remained silent even as Mollie continued to write to him. By the end of her first year of teaching at Wilberforce College, Mollie had resolved to approach the matter head-on. Returning to a pattern established when she was much younger, she first traveled to New York to spend some of her vacation with her mother. Then, with less than 24 hours notice by cablegram, Mollie boarded a train for her father's home in Memphis. As she had hoped, Robert Church met his daughter at the train station with open arms. Before summer's end, he supported her decision to return to work at Wilberforce. It was his first acknowledgment that his adult daughter had ideas of her own. She was indeed a self-described "chip off the old block."[15] Following a second successful year at Wilberforce College, Mollie Church accepted an invitation to spend the summer traveling abroad in the company of a friend. However, plans for the trip, which her father had agreed to pay for, came to a halt when she received a job offer from the "colored" high school in Washington, D.C. In accepting the new position, Mollie Church made a decision that she later described as having "change(d) the entire course of my life."

Founded in the decade after the Civil War and renamed numerous times during the next 80 years, M Street High School was a source of pride for Blacks across the country. As the high school counterpart of Howard University, the school later known as Dunbar High School was unique in the nation. Established with the express intention of preparing more Black Americans for entry into the best Ivy League universities, the school drew a disproportionate number of students from Black upper and middle classes. Staffed by Black administrators and faculty holding college degrees, the institution led by example. The college preparatory curriculum was equivalent to that of the white students in the schools of the district and operated with the approval and active support of the Black elite.[16] Both the reputation of M Street High School and the prospect of living in the nation's capital made the new position especially desirable. Placing her much-desired European travel plans on the back burner, Mollie Church moved to Washington, D.C., to teach Latin at the school. It was there that she also would meet Robert H. Terrell, the man she eventually wed. At the end of her first year in Washington, Mollie eagerly accepted her father's offer to escort her on the delayed trip abroad. Along with organizing the details of the trip, Mollie returned to the routine that had been established with her parents' separation and divorce. Before traveling with her father, she first went to New York to visit her mother and "to purchase what I needed before sailing."[17]

Boarding the steamship *City of Berlin* in the summer of 1888, Mollie and Robert Church arrived in England a week later. For the next three months, father and daughter explored the major cities of Europe in easy companionship. Undaunted by his own lack of formal education, Robert Church matched his daughter's enthusiasm throughout England, Belgium, Switzerland and France. Returning to Paris at the end of the scheduled tour, Robert Church had come to a decision that would have been unlikely for any other "true" Southern gentleman of his era: he would return to the United States alone. Bowing to his daughter's wishes, Church agreed to support Mollie in her desire to live and study abroad for a year. Greeting her father's departure with sadness but "not a tear," Mollie Church was "the happiest girl on earth." Having neither specific plans nor close friends at hand, her idea was simply to "study French, visit the wonderful galleries ... learn something about art, and attend the theaters ... here at last was the realization of those radiant dreams which had filled my head and heart for years."

Once completely on her own in Paris, some dreams were revealed as just that: dreams. Not only was the city more expensive than expected, but "very few American girls went about the city alone." Undaunted and unwilling to bear the expense of hiring a chaperone in order to attend the theater, Mollie devised another plan. Determined to continue studying the French language and culture, she enrolled in a private school for girls and women in Lausanne, Switzerland. In lieu of a hotel, she secured a room for herself in the home of a family that included two daughters close to her own age. In spite of a lack of familiarity with the terrain, Mollie cheerfully made the "daily hike over a young mountain" in order to reach the school.

Almost a year later, still doing exactly what she wanted, she moved on to another country and another language. Now with an interest in studying German, Church made her way to Berlin. This time she encountered challenges she had not met in either Paris or Lausanne. Arriving first in Dresden, she was put off by the large number of American tourists whose presence reaffirmed her choice of Berlin as a more hospitable place to study. She quite simply "knew that a foreign city full of my white countrymen was no place for a colored girl. I was trying to flee from the evils of race prejudice, so depressing in my own country, and it seemed stupid indeed for me to place myself in a position to encounter it abroad."

Arriving in Berlin in December of 1889, Mollie Church found this city also was not completely free of her white American brethren. Attempting to find a stress-free environment, she avoided hotels and settled down in a friendly boarding house. The other lodgers with whom she formed a relaxed relationship included "a tall young German with a magnificent physique ... an interesting little clerk ... and two Hebrew brothers."

Proceeding with her plans to study the native language, Mollie enrolled in one of the few schools open to female students. She also roamed the city of Berlin and the suburbs with the "two brothers," with whom she had formed a close bond.[18] Within a few months, this small social circle grew to include both men and women from as far away as Russia and Belgium. It was a setting in which she was comfortable but not naïve. On receiving a proposal of marriage from a poor but talented musician from Austria, Church expressed both amusement and disgust at what she proclaimed was his search for "a rich American wife."

Counted among the other unexpected surprises was the chance meeting with other Blacks from America. One of several incidents occurred when Will Marion Cook, a musician known to Mollie in the States, spotted her walking down the street. Cook, a composer and violinist who would eventually become well known, had also come to Berlin to study.[19]

Finding obvious comfort in the streets, theaters and schools of a city open to "a colored girl trying to cultivate her mind in a foreign land" did not mean complete freedom from the burden of racial prejudice. Eventually, Mollie was directly confronted with the issue by two white American medical students who had accommodations in the same boarding house she had chosen. Pressuring the landlady to evict their darker countrywoman, the men explained that no decent business in their country would ever serve Blacks. They assured her that no American traveler would even consider her dwelling if it was known that Blacks had ever occupied the residence.

Moving on into a second boarding house, Church found herself welcomed but still uncomfortable. She was more than a little taken aback to find an otherwise-delightful young woman continually expressing a loathing of Jews. Even after several serious discussions, the two women never reached an understanding of their different attitudes.

Before the end of a nearly two-year sojourn, Mollie Church had become adept at making her own way across the terrain and through the cultures of Europe. In letters addressed to her father between September 1888 and May 1890, she was able to put his concerns to rest. Before returning to America, she would serve as a tour guide for her parents as both made their own separate trips abroad. The ex-Mrs. Church, along with Mary's younger brother, Thomas, explored Europe and the Paris Exposition in 1889. Months later, Robert Church arrived in order to escort his daughter home. He, however, arrived with his second wife and their two small children. Placing themselves into the well-seasoned hands of Mary, the reconfigured family visited several European cities. Inevitably venturing into some of the same areas traveled with her mother, Mollie Church had clearly mastered the art of negotiating the tangled pathways of parental divorce, stepmothers and new siblings.[20] Whatever her parents' course of action, Mary Church was not dissuaded from pursuing her own direction in matters of the heart. After experiencing the excitement and freedom of living abroad, returning to M Street High School would seem to offer few challenges. It was the place, however, that opened the door to the next stage of her life. Within a year, a warm relationship with one of her coworkers had evolved into something more.

On October 18, 1891, Mary Church and Robert Herberton Terrell were married in an elaborate ceremony in Memphis, Tennessee. For members of the now-expanded Church family, this occasion was conducted in the same manner as important events of the past. With the expenses of the wedding—including a trousseau—funded by her father, Mary joined her mother on long, pre-wedding shopping excursions in New York. It was apparently understood that Louisa Ayers would not attend her daughter's nuptials; she found her own way to enjoy the festivities. At the very moment the ceremony was taking place, the excluded mother "dressed herself as she would have done if she had actually attended ... and ... imagined ... taking part in it." Unwilling to ignore the situation, the newlyweds ended their elaborate ceremony by boarding a late-night train traveling to New York to visit Louisa Ayers at her home.[21]

In spite of the fractured nature of her own parents' relationship, Mary Church and Robert Terrell were united in contented wedlock for more than 40 years. Even after a decade of marriage, Mary still wrote to her husband, "My own Sweetheart ... It is so blessed to own a man like you." She even managed to sound a bit risqué while keeping him abreast of her speaking engagements across several states: "I could write all night. It's the only way I can be with you all night ... How much better I could rest with you tonight .... Yours Always, Mollie." Robert Terrell was equally affectionate, addressing letters to "My dearest Wife" and sometimes simply "My Darling." Whether ending his letters with "Oceans of love from your devoted husband" or simply "With lots of love," he signed his letters with the intimate name, "Berto."[22]

With her marriage, Mollie Eliza Church began to transform into the Mary Church Terrell found in history books. Two especially treasured wedding gifts provide some insight into the direction her life would begin to take. The gifts, a cream pitcher and a set of oyster forks, were both sterling silver, but each had come from a distinctly different segment of American society. The cream pitcher, a gift from one of the groom's Harvard classmates, had come from T. Jefferson Coolidge, a great-grandson of President Thomas Jefferson. The oyster forks had come from Mary's close childhood friend, Tom Moss. Less than six months after the elaborate Church/Terrell nuptials, Moss, the owner of a store in Memphis, Tennessee, was killed by a white mob. Repeating the scenario that had taken place with Mary's father in 1866, the horde deliberately destroyed Moss's business as well. Terrell felt the loss of her friend for some time and on at least two levels. One was very personal while the other opened up a wider door. Pregnant with her first child, she lamented, "the mob's murder of this friend affected me deeply, and for a long time I could think of nothing else." When the infant died shortly after birth, Terrell reflected, "The more I thought how my depression which was caused by the lynching of Tom Moss ... might have ... affected my unborn child ... the more I became reconciled to what had at first seemed a cruel fate."

When searching for ways to relieve her own pain, Mary Terrell was moved to cast doubt on social institutions and sacred ideas. The viciousness of her friend's death pushed her to "question the Christian religion" and to call for "church militants ... ministers in their pulpits and Christians in their pews" to stem the tide of mob violence against "colored Americans."

Within a five-year period, the Terrells lost three newborn infants, and white violence against Black Americans continued unchecked. The broader questions raised by lynchings and the death of her friend Thomas Moss haunted Mary Terrell for many years. Decades later, it was his memory that fueled her thoughts as she marched alongside other Black anti-lynching protesters: "I thought of the fine boy whom I knew as a girl, who had been brutally lynched when he was a man."[23]

That most white Americans accepted repeated public attacks on Black citizens as normal behavior was an added source of frustration to Terrell and the larger Black community. Reporting on each outrage, the Black press kept readers informed with articles and editorials on incidents often overlooked or discounted by the white media. The frequency with which large crowds gathered to witness acts of torture and mutilation without interference from the law required new ways of calling attention to the atrocities. In reporting on the rampant violence that took place during the 1890s, the Black press began to add graphic images to the written descriptions of lynchings, dismemberment and human bonfires. Newspaper subscribers could, for the first time, view cartoons and illustrations depicting whites as cowards and bloodthirsty killers. Drawings portrayed an impotent or unconcerned "Uncle Sam" failing to protect Black men, women and children.²⁴ Picking up her pen, Terrell joined the war of words leveled against the problem. In spite of professing that "[n]obody wants to know a colored woman's opinion about her own status or that of her group," she seldom hesitated to use her pen in defense of her views.²⁵ When the literary magazine *North American Review* published an article justifying lynching as a necessary means of addressing the "Negro's uncontrollable urge to rape," Terrell immediately drafted a response. After months of near-pleading and numerous rewrites, her rebuttal, "Lynching From a Negro's Point of View," was finally published in June of 1904. Giving specific details of recent incidences in which Black victims were set on fire, dismembered and hanged, Terrell identified racial hatred and the lawlessness of white people as the motivation for "this wild and diabolical carnival of blood." She specifically took Northerners to task for their willingness to believe "the negro's diabolical assaults upon white women are the chief cause of lynching." Leaving no one off the list of culprits, she called attention to "white men who shoot negroes to death and flay them alive, and ... white women who apply flaming torches to their oil-soaked bodies."²⁶

As a member of the Black elite in the nation's capital, Mary Church Terrell fulfilled her expected role by becoming deeply immersed in women's groups and clubs. While good deeds and charitable works replaced paying jobs for middle- and upper-class women regardless of race, an added dimension existed within Black communities throughout the United States. Very real issues of survival and progress of "the race" watered the roots of Black female activities. Across the country, African-American women joined together, originally under the auspices of the church, to address local concerns and needs. Prior to the existence of institutionalized social service agencies, or in the absence of any willing to serve Blacks, their mission was to help the poor and the sick, the orphaned and the aged in their midst. By the 1880s, Black women's organizations could be found in all sections of the country addressing needs as they saw fit. In Knoxville, Tennessee, the Women's Mutual Improvement Club "provided food and clothing for the needy," while a group with a similar name in Selma, Alabama, "paid the tuition of ... children of widowed mothers in schools of the city." In Raleigh, North Carolina, a group called the "Tent Sisters" was able to support a home for the aged with the pledge of 25 cents a year from 250 women. They also agreed to each contribute one pound of food per month to sustain the home's residents. Rhode Island's working women also pooled their resources but focused their attention in another direction. They wished to "loan money and invest in real estate." Given the disproportionate number of educated Black women residing in the nation's capital, the work of the Colored Women's League of Washington, D.C. followed an expected path. The group, of which Mary Terrell was a founding member, pledged to pay the tuition for two nurses-in-training in the medical department at Howard University. Clubwomen also agreed to provide one-half of the salary needed to secure the services of a kindergarten teacher. In an even more ambitious undertaking, the women organized a trade school where 88 students were paid "a small sum to keep up their interest."[27] By the closing decade of the nineteenth century, Black women were more than adept at running their own groups and organizations. They depended neither on the blessings of the church nor the direction of men. From this position, they debated and engaged broader social questions such as temperance and suffrage, as well as the ongoing and socially sanctioned mob violence against Blacks.

With time, the wisdom and benefits of uniting individual women's groups across the country under one national banner overwhelmed internal opposition. Demonstrating their own skills and commitment, a core group took on the arduous task of linking nearly 200 independent Black women's associations. In 1896, in spite of vast geographical distances, as well as social and political differences, Mary Church Terrell emerged as the first elected president of the National Association of Colored Women. One of several women who would have been well-suited for the position, Terrell had education, social status and a strong record of active involvement in women's organizations. In the year prior to her election, Mary had been appointed the first Black female on the Board of Education in Washington, D.C. Centered in the nation's capital, the appointment was a matter of racial pride across the country. In addition, the new president of this new organization had traveled throughout the North and South giving speeches on issues of race and gender. Well-suited to the task of leading the fledgling new association, Terrell served two terms at the helm and was finally elected honorary president for life.[28] Whether club members or not, African American women would generally have found little reason to question her ability to represent the race anywhere in the world. It was primarily this purpose that would stimulate Terrell's travels abroad in the second stage of her life.

By 1904, the year that Mary Terrell received an invitation from the International Congress of Women to deliver a speech in Germany, her life had become somewhat more complicated. Now 41 years old and the mother of a six-year-old child, Mary was also faced with a reality that might have been invisible to others but familiar among the Black elite. The Terrells and others had a family income *"that was not very large ... and living expenses by no means small."* In fact, high-status, highly visible occupations were seldom accompanied by commensurate wages. Even a degree from Harvard did not ensure that Robert Terrell was rewarded with the same salary as that of similarly educated white males. Many middle- and upper-class Blacks maintained their economic position by holding two or more jobs at the same time. During his career, Robert held dual positions as a high school principal and a member of Washington, D.C.'s Board of Trades. After President Taft appointed him a Justice of the Municipal Court in 1910, Terrell also held a faculty position at Howard University School of Law. For some time, he also maintained a career as a practicing attorney. The family also reaped financial gain from the "activities" of Mary Terrell. Although not considered "work" by the society at large, Robert's much-sought-after spouse brought in speaking fees that provided more than social capital. Writing to her husband from one of her multistate speaking tours, Mary Terrell managed to weave family and financial matters neatly together:

> I think that remaining in Chicago will mean $20.00 extra in money ... still I ask myself whether earning $20.00 should have tempted me to stay away from you seven whole days ... I hope I shall do as well in Columbus Junction, Iowa as I did in Decatur ... try to keep Phyllis from eating too much meat and have her eat lightly at night. ... Kiss her and yourself thousands of times for me and give my love to Mother.

It cannot be doubted that Mary Terrell enjoyed the exposure and status that came with her role as a much-admired public figure, but she was pragmatic as well. While "not on the platform to make money," she did not deny that "I needed money, of course, and was glad to get it."[29]

The International Congress of Women was one of the earliest multinational gatherings organized by women. Between 1878 and 1921, women created at least eight multinational meetings. They came together in various cities throughout Europe and North America to discuss a wide range of social issues, including women's rights.
In spite of the concerns that travel to Europe generated, both the Church and Terrell clans were anxious to have one of their own "represent the Negro abroad."

The very real problem of funding the trip was solved when Robert Church once again agreed to finance his daughter's journey. When Mary's husband and mother both agreed to assist with childcare, the final obstacles were removed. The Mary Church Terrell who arrived in Germany in 1904 was a more matured version of the Mollie Church of 1888. Still eager to thrust herself into unfamiliar social and cultural environments, she now did so armed with a broader mission. Now she traveled across the world to "present the facts ... creditable to colored women of the United States ... and to enlighten ... my friends across the sea upon the condition of the race problem ... as it really is." Although not the only American woman to attend the conference, she arrived in Berlin to find herself the only delegate "who had a drop of African blood in her veins." Distinguishing herself even further, Terrell was the sole speaker from England or the United States able to deliver her remarks in any language but her own. After hearing German women complain that delegates from English-speaking countries had not bothered to have their papers translated, it became clear that even those familiar with English would not be able to understand the formal conference communication. Terrell hurriedly rewrote her remarks. Commandeering the assistance of several native Germans, she practiced her pronunciation and delivered her paper to the apparent appreciation of the crowd. Her second paper, given later the same day, was delivered entirely in French.[30]

In the years that separated Terrell's first and second trips abroad, a lifetime of changes had taken place. One remaining constant was her desire to experience life unhampered by race. Her feelings were evident in an article written for the literary journal *The Voice of the Negro*. Meetings with titled Europeans and elegant surroundings were described with obvious enjoyment, but Mary Terrell also repeatedly stressed to readers that the ugly specter of race did not bar Blacks from any public place. Writing for an audience with minimal, if any, possibility of traveling abroad, Terrell described what most could not ever hope to see: "In France there is absolutely no prejudice .... so far as I was able to ascertain ... intermarriage between black and white ... causes no commotion at all. In Germany there seems to be no prejudice based on ... color. It is conceivable that a colored man of ability might become an officer in the German army, whereas ... could not ... be attained by a Jew." Evaluating somewhat more familiar territory, she reserved her most caustic comments for the British:

> England's career in South Africa has not been good for her morals, I fear. The feeling in general ... so far as I could glean from conversations with representative English people ... the Lord God of Hosts has ordained that the pale-faced Caucasian should rule over all the peoples of the face of the earth and possess the fullness thereof, and many of their cousins on this side of the water have been deluded into believing the same thing.

Following her 6,000-mile journey, Mary Terrell returned to the United States with a clearly articulated and wide-ranging commitment to her work:

> [I]f it was possible for me to interest even a few people in foreign lands in the struggle which the women as well as the men of my race are making to rise from the degradation and ignorance forced upon them for nearly 300 years, my mission was gloriously fulfilled. ... I have made up my mind therefore, that for the rest of my natural life, I shall devote as much of my time and strength as I can to enlightening my friends across the sea upon the condition of the race problem in the United States, as it really is.[31]

Another decade and a half would pass before Terrell would manage to carry the message abroad once again. This time, she would do so as a member and officer of the Women's International League for Peace and Freedom. Making her way into war-torn Europe in 1919, she arrived in Zurich, Switzerland. As with her previous trip to Berlin, she observed that "women from all over the white world were present ... after an unspeakable world war .... there was not a single delegate from Japan, China, India or from any other country whose inhabitants were not white."[32] Undaunted by having to represent all the "non-white countries in the world," Terrell placed the treatment of Blacks in America at the center of the discussion on world peace. She deftly informed her audience that thousands of "colored" soldiers had fought in Europe. They had "crossed the sea to make the world safe for democracy ... for freedom for others which in some sections of their own country they themselves did not enjoy." Her listeners were boldly cautioned, "You may talk about permanent peace until doomsday ... but the world will never have it til the dark races are given a square deal."[33] Mary had traveled to Switzerland alone, but her message had sprung from a broader base. It represented a strain of Black female global consciousness that was evident even as the First World War drew to an end. Women such as Delilah Beasley had actively participated in the California branch of the League of Nations Association. In other areas of the country, women had circulated petitions in support of the Geneva Disarmament Conference. Black women's propensity to reshape large ideas and global concerns to fit the needs of their own lives led to the creation of the International Council of Women of the Darker Races in 1922. The short-lived but extremely ambitious ICWDR garnered the support of Terrell, along with Mary Murray Washington, the wife of Booker T. Washington, and Addie Hunton. Setting their own ambitious goals, the women were desirous of learning and teaching more about Africa and other dark peoples of the world. Washington urged that members "study any … or all questions in a systematic way, relative to the darker races. No matter whether these … are races willing to be affiliated with us or not. You probably already know the attitude of both Japan and China and the Indians, and Hindoos too, with reference to the American Negro, but … this makes little or no difference."[34]

The decade of the 1930s may have afforded Mary Terrell her last opportunities, or perhaps desire, for foreign travel. In an effort to expose her daughter Phyllis to some of the same opportunities she had enjoyed, the two set sail for Europe in June of 1930. At 67 years of age, Mary Church Terrell retraced her earlier footsteps now with her adult offspring in tow. Seven years later, in her mid-70s, she was still energized enough to sail across the ocean yet again. This time, she journeyed alone to London to deliver a paper before the International Assembly of the World Fellowship of Faiths. The gathering provided at least two extraordinary opportunities: she met Haile Selassie, the exiled Emperor of Ethiopia, as well as East Indian protesters. The latter group was of special interest to her "because the attitude of the English toward that dark race is exactly like that of the dominant race in this country toward colored people. If you had closed your eyes and listened to the speeches of protest made … you might easily have thought you were listening to a colored man describing the conditions in the United States."[35] Even after she ceased to travel abroad, Mary Terrell would both boast and complain in her autobiography:

> I can dance as long and as well as I ever did, although I get very few chances to do so. There seems to be a sort of a tradition that after a woman reaches a certain age she should not want to … she should not be allowed … I believe if a woman could dance or swim a half hour every day, her span of life would be greatly

lengthened, her health ... improved and the joy of living decidedly increased.[36]

By 1949, there was evidence that such a progressive approach to healthy living was worth the effort. When she was well into her 80s, Mary Terrell was offered and accepted leadership positions of two major but very different civil rights causes. Taken together, the cases illustrate the broad base and lethal dimensions of racial antipathy during the time period. They are also indications of Terrell's readiness to add confrontation and civil disobedience to her lifelong stock of resistance techniques.

At one end of the spectrum, the Rosa Lee Ingram case was a fight to save the life and restore the freedom of a Black female sharecropper and two of her 12 children, who had been sentenced to death by the state of Georgia. Of less immediate dire consequences, the second cause was a battle to end discrimination against Blacks in restaurants in the nation's capital. Each case generated public outcry and resistance prior to Terrell's involvement. Her task was to maintain and expand waning public and political interest in the issues.[37] Given broad name recognition along with proven organizational skills, Mary Terrell's leadership of the National Committee to Free the Ingram Family was a logical choice. Using tactics gleaned from decades of work in women's groups, she devised a plan of action. Drawing attention to Rosa Ingram as a mother, committee members visited her and her sons in prison. In addition, they visited and made provisions for Mrs. Ingram's younger children. Mother's Day rallies were organized in Black churches, postcards adorned with her image were distributed and petitions requesting federal investigation of the case were collected. In spite of her age, Terrell personally led a NCFIF committee in delivering petitions to the White House and requesting a meeting with President Harry S. Truman. In December 1953, she led a group of 60 women in a prayer meeting on the steps of the Georgia State Capital building, followed by a meeting with the governor. Their death sentences having been commuted to life imprisonment in 1948, Mrs. Ingram and her sons would finally gain parole in 1959.

Between discussions with the Justice Department Division of Civil Rights and lodging complaints with the United Nations, Terrell became deeply involved in a second struggle that was much closer to home. While Blacks in the nation's capital may have lived with less fear of daily and rampant anti-Black violence than those in Georgia, they did not escape white hostility, aggression and brutality. Traditionally, the few existing segregation laws focused on schools, recreational facilities and agencies of the federal government. Inexplicably, streetcars and public libraries did not require complete separation of the races. Treatment in stores and eating establishments could vary, depending on business owners and their employees. The most critical form of discrimination faced by all segments of the African American community was in the area of employment. As early as 1907, Mary Terrell found reason to doubt Washington, D.C.'s reputation as "the Colored Man's Paradise." In her estimation, "In Washington the colored laborer's path to a decent livelihood is by no means smooth …. colored men must remain idle, unless the supply of white men is too small." Three decades later, she had reason to continue:

> And yet, colored people are constantly being … blamed in the National Capital because so many of them are on relief. … colored men are not given jobs, even when there are not enough white men to fill them, and colored women know that the Employment Center wants only white women for all types of hotel and restaurant work, it is difficult, if not impossible, for many of them to earn their living, They must either go on relief or let their families … starve.

Black Washingtonians' resistance to ill-treatment ran the gamut from appealing to the judicial systems to armed defense. The latter came into play during the 1919 race riot, when Blacks used guns, knives and bricks to defend their neighborhoods against armed white mobs.[38] By the mid-1930s, the scattered use of boycotts and picket lines was added to the arsenal of weaponry used by Blacks protesting unequal treatment.

In 1949, Mary Church Terrell was asked to serve as coordinator for a broad-based, citywide anti-discrimination committee. Composed of dozens of separate groups and organizations, the structure and purpose of the Committee for the Enforcement of the District of Columbia Anti-Discrimination Laws (CEDCADL) resonated with Terrell. As an integrationist, she had used speeches, writings and exemplary public behavior to persuade, shame and pester her opposition. In her mid-80s, without disavowing other previous forms of resistance, Terrell embraced more active and direct forms of protest. Along with three other members of the CEDCADL, she filed a test case after the group was refused service in a restaurant. No longer satisfied to wait for the courts to render a decision, Terrell and her committee petitioned President Eisenhower and urged Blacks to direct action as well. Donning hat, purse and cane, 87-year-old Mary Church Terrell joined her first picket lines. When the court's ruling was handed down three years later, Blacks had won the legal right to be served at all public eating-places in the nation's capital. With restrained jubilation, Terrell cautioned, "Laws ... can be lost again."[39]

A little more than a year later, Mary Church Terrell's life came to an end. Dying of undisclosed causes on July 24, 1956, she had witnessed the end of human bondage and the beginning of the end of legal racial segregation. Just two months after the Supreme Court passage of *Brown v. Board of Education*, she was laid to rest in the Lincoln Memorial Cemetery.

Chapter 4

Beginning life as an indulged, self-possessed young woman of privilege, Terrell chose a path ever at odds with a world unclear of just how much freedom would be allowed to those of her kind. During nine decades of life, she traveled great distances both at home and abroad to emerge as a formidable fighter in the battle for civil rights and social reform.

Notes

Introduction

1. Bess Beatty, *Traveling Beyond Her Sphere: American Women on the Grand Tour, 1814–1914*, (Washington DC: New Academia Publishing, 2016). See esp. the "Prelude."
2. David Eltis, "The Age and Sex of Africans in the Transatlantic Slave Trade," in *The Rise of African Slavery in the Americas*, (Cambridge: Cambridge University Press, 2000), 285–92; David Eltis and Stanley L. Engerman, "Fluctuations in Sex and Age Ratios in the Transatlantic Slave Trade, 1663–1864," *The Economic History Review* 46, no. 2 (1993): 308–23; Barbara Bush, "'Daughters of Injur'd Africk': African Women and the Transatlantic Slave Trade," *Womens History Review* 17, no. 5 (2008): 673–98, accessed September 26, 2013.
3. Thomas Chandler Haliburton. *The Letter-Bag of the Great Western, or, Life in a Steamer* Reprint ed. (London: David Bryce, 1853), 181–187; see Elizabeth Anne Pryor, "'Jim Crow' Cars, Passport Denials and Atlantic Crossings: African-American Travel, Protest and Citizenship at Home and Abroad, 1827–1865," (PhD diss., University of California, Santa Barbara, 2008), 177–187.
4. Ruthella Mory Bibbins, *Mammy 'Mongst the Wild Nations of Europe*, (New York: Frederick A. Stokes, 1904), 2, 236. For similar images of mammys who remain at home see Gertrude Langhorne, *Mammy's Letters*, (Macon, GA: J.W. Burke Company, 1922); Emma Speed Sampson, *Mammy's White Folks*, (Chicago: Reilly & Lee, 1919).
5. Scholars still debate the possibility that Remond may have returned to the United States for a short visit in 1866. See Sibyl Ventress Brownlee, "Out Of The Abundance Of The Heart; Sarah Ann Parker Remond's Quest For Freedom," (PhD diss., University of Massachusetts, 1997), 152–3.

6 As a colonial power, France wrung enormous wealth from the labor of Africans imported to, and enslaved on, the island of Haiti. The brute force required in the production of sugar, rum, cotton, tobacco and indigo led to slave revolts. After more than a century under French rule, freedom was gained through a series of slave revolts and finally outright armed rebellion. As a result, Haiti became the first Independent Black Republic in the Western Hemisphere. Between 1889 and 1891, Frederick Douglass served as the second African American U.S. Minister to Haiti.

7 Narrative of the Life and Travels of Mrs. Nancy Prince. 2 ed. Boston, 1853. Reprinted in Bert James Loewenberg and Ruth Bogin. Black Women In Nineteenth-Century American Life: Their Words, Their Thoughts, Their Feelings. Pennsylvania University Press. 1976. Pg. 206. Expanded versions of the narrative were printed 1853 and 1856; Carla Peterson. "Colored Tourist" : Nancy Prince, Mary Ann Shadd Cary, Ethnographic Writing, and the Question of Home' in " Doers of the Word" African American Women Speakers and Writers In The North {1830–1880}. Rutgers University Press, 1998. For additional information on the early Black presence in Russia, see Allison Blakely. "The Negro in Imperial Russia. 'Journal of Negro History 61 (October 1976}; Mina Curtiss "Some American Negroes in Russia in the 19th Century." Massachusetts Review Spring 1968. Pg. 268-278.

8 Zilpha Elaw, *Memoirs Of The Life, Religious Experience, Ministerial Travels and Labours Of Mrs. Zilpha Elaw, An American Female of Colour: Together with Some Account of the Great Religious Revivals in America [Written by Herself]*, (London, 1846), 137–139, 158. Reprinted in William L. Andrews, *Sisters of the Spirit: Three Black Women's Autobiographies of the Nineteenth Century*, (Indiana University Press, 1986).

9 Elaw, *Memoirs of the Life*, 49–160. Until recently scholars have had reason to believe that Elaw returned to the U.S., died and was buried there. More current and exhaustive research conducted by Elizabeth Anne Pryor documents Elaw's remarriage in 1850 in London to Ralph Bressy Shum. Zilpha Elaw Shum died in London in 1873. See Pryor, *African American Travel, Protest and*

Citizenship, 229–233; Amanda Smith, *An Autobiography. The Story of the Lord's Dealings with Mrs. Amanda Smith the Colored Evangelist; Containing an Account of Her Life Work of Faith, and Her Travels in America, England, Ireland, Scotland, India, and Africa, as an Independent Missionary*, (1893), Reprint, (New York: Oxford University Press, 1988).

10   See letter to American Missionary Association, April 11, 1854. Reprinted in Ellen NicKenzie Lawson with Marlene D. Merrill, *The Three Sarahs: Documents of Antebellum Black College Women*, (Edwin Mellen Press, 1984), 36–37.

11   Mary Helen Washington, "A Voice From The South," in Joan R. Sherman, ed. *Library of Nineteenth Century Black Women Writers*. (1988), xxxi.

12   Debra Newman Ham, *A Colored Woman In a White World, Mary Church Terrell*, (Humanity Books, 2005), 46.

Chapter 1

1   Eric Taylor identified 493 cases of shipboard rebellion. He described this form of resistance as "far more than occasional." See Eric Robert Taylor, *If We Must Die: Shipboard Insurrections in the Era of the Atlantic Slave Trade*, (Louisiana State University Press, 2006), 5–9. See especially "Chronology of Shipboard Slave Revolts, 1509–1865," 179–213. For slightly different numbers see David Eltis *et al.*, *The Trans-Atlantic Slave Trade: A Database on CD-ROM*, (Cambridge University Press, 1999).

2   Benjamin N. Lawrance, *Amistad's Orphans: An Atlantic Story of Children, Slavery, and Smuggling*, (Yale University Press, 2014), 28-3, 35–36; Donald D. Wax, "A Philadelphia Surgeons Slaving Voyage to Africa, 1749–1751," *Pennsylvania Magazine of History and Biography*, XCII, no. 4 (Oct. 1968): 465–493; Erik J.W. Hofstee, "The Great Divide: Aspects of the Social History of the Middle Passage in the Transatlantic Slave Trade," (PhD diss., Michigan State University, 2001), Chapter 2 "Infants and Children" especially see 5, 69, 83; Elizabeth Donnan, *Documents Illustrative of the History of the Slave Trade in America*, (Octagon Books, 1965), 2:327, 584–85.

3   Sharla M. Fett, *Recaptured Africans: Surviving Slave Ships, Detention, And Dislocation In The Final Years Of the Slave Trade*, (University of North Carolina Press, 2017), 8.
4   David Turnbull, *Travels in the West: Cuba, with Notices of Porto Rico and the Slave Trade*, (London: Longman, Orme, Brown, Green, and Longman, 1840), 57–61.
5   In testimony before the U.S. District Court Judge Andrew T. Judson, Don Jose Ruiz described the cabin boy as African by birth "but had lived a long time in Cuba." The boy is later described as "Creole, born in Spain." See John Warner Barber, *A History of the Amistad Captives: Being a Circumstantial Account of the Capture of the Spanish Schooner Amistad, by the Africans on Board: Their Voyage, and Capture near Long Island, New York: With Biographical Sketches of Each of the Surviving Africans: Also, an Account of the Trials Had on Their Case, Before the District and Circuit Courts of the United States, for the District of Connecticut*, (E.L. & J.W. Barber Hitchcock and Stafford Printers, 1840), 6–7, 24.
6   *New York Advertiser and Express*, Aug. 24, 1839; *New York Morning Herald*, Sept. 9, 1839. On the many variations of Cinquez's name see Iyunolu Folayan Osagie, *The Amistad Revolt: Memory, Slavery, And The Politics of Identity In The United States And Sierra Leone*, (University of Georgia Press, 2000), 140–141; Also see *The Colored American*, "On Cinques" Oct. 19, 1839, 1.
7   Barber, 8, 16.
8   The first foreign students to attend college in America included non-Europeans. The earliest foreign students that can be documented include Fernando Bolivar from Venezuela, who attended the University of Virginia in 1826; Yung Wink, also known as Rong Hong Hung, from China, who attended Yale University in 1854; Niijima Jo (a.k.a. Joseph Hardy) Neesims from Japan, who attended Amherst College in the 1870s; and Mario Garcia Menocol from Cuba, who attended Cornell University in 1888. In 1903, through a special government program, 100 students were brought to the United States from the Philippines, eight of whom were female. Following in the footsteps of Mar'gru, Dr. Honoria Acosta-Sisson received her medical degree from University of Pennsylvania in 1909. Returning to her country, Acosta became the first female physician in the Philippines. Menocol

became president of Cuba while Tong Shao-yi became prime minister of the Chinese Republic. Chan Tien-Yu would eventually design and build the famous Peking-Kalgan Railway system, the first built completely by Chinese labor and without any foreign assistance. See Teresa Brawner Bevis and Christopher J. Lucas, *International Students in American Colleges and Universities: A History*, (Palgrave Macmillan, 2007). See esp. "Chapter 2" especially, 51; Joseph Agris, "'Honoria Acosta Sison,' Pioneer Gynecologist and Obstetrician." *Journal of Dermatology, Surgery and Oncology* 6, no. 3 (March 1980): 178.

9   As in other sections of the country, slaveholders in Connecticut did not release their hold on unpaid labor easily. Attempts to hold onto their human chattel or even pass them on to heirs continued for a time after passage of legal statutes. However, as early as 1788, slaves and their supporters were filing freedom petitions, and by 1841, Connecticut Blacks were lobbying for the right to vote. See Joanne Pope Melish, *Disowning Slavery: Gradual Emancipation and Race in New England, 1780–1869*, (Cornell University Press, 1998). See esp. Chapter 3, "'Slaves of the Community': Gradual Emancipation in Practice"; "Right of Suffrage," *Colored American*, June 12, 1841; Willian D. Piersen, *The Development of an Afro-American Subculture in Eighteenth-Century New England*, (University of Massachusetts, 1988). In 1840, Blacks represented 2.6 percent of Connecticut's population and declined to 2.1 within 10 years. Robert Austin Warner, *New Haven Negroes: A Social History*, (1940; repr., Arno Press, 1969), 301. For examples of freedom petitions, see "Petition of 1788 by Slaves of New Haven" and "Petition of 1779 by Slaves of Fairfield County," *Connecticut State Library Archives of Revolution War Papers*, series 1, vol. 37, document 232, document 251; Helen Tunnicliff Catterall, "Connecticut Cases," *Judicial Cases Concerning American Slavery and the Negro* 1V (Octagon Press, 1968): 419, 421, 522, 423, 433–436.

10 Richard Hofstader and Michael Wallace, eds., *American Violence: A Documentary History*, (1971), 477–478.

11 William C. Fowler, *The Historical Status of The Negro In Connecticut: A Paper Read Before The New Haven Colony Historical Society*, (Walker, Evans & Cogswell Co, 1901), 39; Philip S. Foner and

Josephine F. Pacheco, *Three Who Dared: Prudence Crandall, Margaret Douglass, Myrtilla Miner, Champions of Antebellum Black Education*, (Westport Connecticut: Greenwood Press, 1984), 5–46.

12 Carl E. Prince, "'The Great Riot Year': Jacksonian Democracy and Patterns of Violence in 1834," *Journal of the Early Republic* 5, no. 1 (Spring 1985): 1–20; David Grimsted, "Rioting in its Jacksonian Setting," *American Historical Review* 77, no. 2 (1972): 361–97; Alfred A. Knopf "Murder of Lovejoy" *American Violence: A Documentary History*, eds. Richard Hofstadter & Michael Wallace, (1970), 407–409.

13 Lewis Tappan (1788–1873) was deeply religious and also a merchant, publisher and financier. He and his brother Arthur supported a wide range of social reform issues including boarding houses for prostitutes, institutes for the "deaf and dumb," insane, indigent boys, hospitals, savings institutions for the poor and the American Bible Society. Lewis Tappan also edited an antislavery magazine for children and founded the New York Journal of Commerce, as well as the first credit rating system in the country. His "Mercantile Agency" evolved to become what is currently known as Dun and Bradstreet. Weaving his Christian faith throughout all of his endeavors Tappan used the *Bible* to challenge fellow believers who chose to support slavery. Bertram Wyatt-Brown, *Lewis Tappan and the Evangelical War Against Slavery*, (Case Western Reserve University, 1969). See esp. chapters 5, 6, 11, 12. Also, Bertram Wyatt-Brown "Three Generations of Yankee Parenthood: The Tappan Family, A Case Study of Antebellum Nurture." *Illinois Quarterly* 38, no.1 (Fall 1975): 11–28; Wyatt-Brown, "God and Dun and Bradstreet, 1841–1851," *Business History Review*, (XL Winter, 1967); Annie Heloise Abel & Frank J. Klingberg, *A Side-Light On Anglo-American Relations, 1839–1858...Furnished by the Correspondence of Lewis Tappan and Others With The British and Foreign Anti-Slavery Society*, (Association For The Study of Negro Life and History, Inc., 1927), 60–63; 69–70.

14 Joshua Leavitt was the editor of an abolitionist newspaper in New York, and Simeon Jocelyn was the white minister of the first Black church in New Haven, Connecticut. *The Emancipator*, Sept. 4, 1839; Roy E. Finkenbine, "The Symbolism of Slave

Mutiny: Black Abolitionist Responses to the Amistad and Creole Incidents," *Rebellion Repression Reinvention: Mutiny in Comparative Perspective*, ed. Jane Hathaway, (Praeger, 2001), 233–252.

15 The African interpreters were John Ferry, James Covey and Charles Pratt. Covey and Pratt were employed aboard the British warship *Buzzard*. See Howard Jones, *Mutiny On The Amistad*, (Oxford University Press, 1987), 41–42; Maggie Montesinos Sale, *The Slumbering Volcano: American Slave Ship Revolts and the Production of Rebellious Masculinity*, (Duke University Press, 1997), 86–87.

16 Osagie, *The Amistad Revolt*, 9–18; Howard Jones, *Mutiny On The Amistad: The Saga of a Slave Revolt and Its Impact on American Abolition, Law, and Diplomacy*, (Oxford University Press, 1987). See esp. chapters 4–10. For discussion of the seriousness of Adams' charges of collusion between the White House and the Government of Spain see pg. 111–119 and 175–182; John Quincy Adams, *Arguments of John Quincy Adams, before the Supreme Court of the United States, in the Case of the United States, Appellants vs. Cinque and Other Africans, Captured in the Schooner Amistad*, (1841; repr., The Basic Afro-American Reprint Library, N.Y.: Arno Press, 1969).

17 *Emancipator*, New York, Sept. 19, 1839 & Sept. 26, 1839; *New York Journal of Commerce*, Sept. 10, 1839.

18 Although his many good works and businesses kept him away from his own children a great deal of the time, Lewis Tappan appeared to be sensitive to the precarious nature of Black children's lives. In at least two instances he involved himself in their rescue, once in 1853 and again in 1855. In the latter instance, Tappan and his wife hide a small girl in their Brooklyn home until she could be "forwarded" on with a Black minister to join her parents in Canada. Tappan also aided Antonio, the slave cabin boy from *La Amistad* in his flight to Canada. Wyatt-Brown, *Lewis Tappan Evangelical War*. 212–216; *Anti-Slavery* 1, Aug. 1, 1853, 169–72 and Sept. 1, 1853, 193–99. Jones, *Mutiny On The Amistad*, 200. It remains unclear why Mar'gru was given the last name Kinson and Kapli the boy continued to be called Kapli; Ellen NicKenzie Lawson & Marlene D. Merrill, *The Three*

Sarahs: Documents Of Antebellum Black College Women, (Edwin Mellen, 1984), 9; Clara Merritt DeBoer, *Be Jubilant My Feet: African American Abolitionists In The American Missionary Association, 1839–1861*, (Garland, 1994), 107.

[19] *Colored American*, Sept. 28, Oct. 19, Nov. 2, 1839; May 23, 1840; Mar. 27, 1841.

[20] "Meetings Of The Liberated Africans" *Colored American*, May 22, 1841; "The Amistad Captives," *Chambers Edinburgh Journal*, Jun. 25,1842, 180–181; Mifflin Wistar Gibbs, *Shadow And Light: An Autobiography With Reminiscences Of The Last And Present Century*, (University of Nebraska Press, 1995), 29–30.

[21] Roy E. Finkenbine "The Symbolism of Slave Mutiny: Black abolitionist Responses to the Amistad and Creole Incidents," *Rebellion, Repression Reinvention: Mutiny in Comparative Perspective*, ed. Jane Hathaway, (Praeger, 2001), 240.

[22] *Liberator*, Dec. 3, 1841; *Colored American*, May 8, May 22, 1841.

[23] Finkenbine, 240–242.

[24] For the Union Missionary Society see "The Amistad Case and the Union Missionary Society" *Be Jubilant My Feet: African American Abolitionist In The American Missionary Association, 1839–1861*, ed. Clara Merritt DeBoer, (Garland, 1994).

[25] Edward Scobie, "The Black Poor And The Sierra Leone Settlement" *Black in Black Britannia: A History of Blacks in Britain*, (Johnson Publishing, Inc., 1972), 62–75; Included among the Black Americans from Nova Scotia was runaway slave, Mary Perth, who was born around 1740 in the colony of Norfolk, Virginia. During the wartime scrimmages between British and American forces, Perth escaped with her daughter and two additional children. Along with thousands of others, she made her way to New York, which was in British hands in 1776. Within a few years, the group was evacuated to Nova Scotia and finally shipped to Sierra Leone. In Freetown she farmed, ran boarding houses, spent a few years in England, married a second husband and disappeared from public record. Mary Louise Clifford, *From Slavery to Freetown: Black Loyalist After the American Revolution*, (McFarland & Company, 1999), 9–14, 29–31, 36–39, 176–177.

[26] Osagie, 59–68; for a list of the 10 remaining captives see DeBoer, 106.

27 Marlene D. Merrill, "Sarah Mar'gru Kinson: The Two Worlds of an Amistad Captive," *Oberlin Historical and Improvement Organization*, (2003), 5. http://www.oberlin.edu/external/EOG/Kinson/Kinson.html.

28 Stanton would go on to become the first Black woman to complete a four-year course of study at an American college or university. *Oberlin College Archives*, (Lawson-Merrll Papers, 1978–1983).

29 The first Black male student enrolled at Oberlin in 1835, followed two years later by Harriet Hunter, the first Black female. Carol Lasser, "Enacting Emancipation: African American Women Abolitionists at Oberlin College and the Quest for Empowerment, Equality, and Respectability," *Women's Rights and Transatlantic Antislavery in the Era of Emancipation*, eds. Kathryn Kish Sklar and James Brewer Stewart, (Yale University Press, 2007), 325; Ellen NicKenzie Lawson with Marlene D. Merrill, *The Three Sarahs: Documents Of Antebellum Black College Women*, (Edwin Mellen Press, 1984), 13–16.

30 Lasser, 319–320, 327–333.

31 Letter dated Oct. 25, 1847, "To Mr. Tappan from Laurette Branch." *American Missionary Association Papers*, (New Orleans: Amistad Research Center, Tulane University).

32 *The Three Sarahs*, 14–15; Letters, S.M. Kinson to Tappan, May, 1847; and S.M. Kinson to George Whipple, Dec., 1847, Kinson File, *American Missionary Association Papers*, (New Orleans Louisiana: Amistad Research Center).

33 Sarah was not the only Black female student whose behavior caused comment. On more than one occasion, Black women students challenged rules and demonstrated their own notions of what could be expected from respectable young ladies of color. See Lasser, 329–333.

34 Lasser, 327; "Report of a Female Moral Reform Society. First Annual Meeting New York Female Reform Society," May 15, 1835, Transcription of Primary Sources. Document found on website *Teach U. S. History*.

35 Marlene D. Merrill, "Sarah Mar'gru Kinson: The Two Worlds of an Amistad Captive," (Oberlin Historical and Improvement Organization, 2003), 7; See letter from Mrs. M.P. Dascomb to

Lewis Tappan Esq. *AMA Archives*, Sarah Kinson Collection, folder 104286, Oct. 25, 1847, (Amistad Research Center, Tulane University); Frederick Douglass, *Autobiographies: Narratives of the Life of Frederick Douglass, an American Slave; My Bondage And My Freedom; Life and Times of Frederick Douglass*. (1994), 266–67.

36   *The Three Sarahs*, 30–31.

37   Letter from Sarah Mar'gru dated Dec. 18, 1847, repr. in *The Three Sarahs*, 27–30; the death of Maria the other young girl aboard *La Amistad* was reported to have taken place in 1857. While the exact death date of Ka-li, the young boy captive, is not known, letters from the mission back to the United States indicate that he was taken prisoner in a dispute between tribes in the late 1840s. See DeBoer, *Be Jubilant My Feet*, 112; Osagie, 65.

38   DeBoer, 106, 117; *The Three Sarahs*, 18.

39   Letter from Sarah to Lewis Tappan, dated Jan. 2, 1851, repr. in *The Three Sarahs*, 32–33.

40   Letter dated Apr. 11, 1854 in *The Three Sarahs*, 36–37.

41   Ibid. Sarah Mar'gru to George Whipple, 38; Also see letters 26, 33, 34.

Chapter 2

1   *Soulby's Ulverston Advertiser*, (Ulverston, England) January 17, 1861.

2   Sibyl Ventress Brownlee, "Out of the Abundance of the Heart: Sarah Ann Parker Remond's Quest for Freedom," (PhD diss., University of Massachusetts Amherst, 1997), 81. For conflicting date of birth see Dorothy B. Porter, "Sarah Parker Remond, Abolitionist and Physician," *Journal of Negro History* 20, no. 1 (January 1935); and Darlene Clark Hine, ed., *Black Women in America: An Historical Encyclopedia*, vol. 2, 972.

3   Arthur O. White, "Salem's Antebellum Black Community: Seedbed of the School Integration Movement," *Essex Institute Historical Collection*, April 1972, vol. CVIII, 99–101, 105–106.

4   Dorothy Burnett Porter, *The Remonds of Salem Massachusetts: A Nineteenth Century Family Revisited* (American Antiquarian Society, 1985), 261. Also see Dorothy Sterling, *We Are Your Sisters: Black Women in the Nineteenth Century* (Norton, 1984), 108–109;

William Piersen, *Black Yankees: The Development of an Afro-American Subculture in Eighteenth Century New England* (University of Massachusetts, 1988), 118.

5   Porter, 262–267, 272; see also: Gloria C. Oden, "The Journal of Charlotte L. Forten: The Salem-Philadelphia Years Reexamined," *Black Women in United States History*, ed. Darlene Clark Hine, vol. 3, 128–129.

6   The Remond children included: Nancy 1809, Charles 1810, John Lenox, Susan 1814, Cecelia 1816, unnamed male died at birth, 1817, Maritche Juan 1817, Mary 1821, Sarah Parker 1824, and Caroline 1826. See Brownlee, 47–48; and Oden 125–136.

7   *Salem Observer*, vol. 4, no. 1, January 1828.

8   Sarah Parker Remond, autobiographical sketch in Matthew Davenport Hill, *Our Exemplars, Poor and rich: Biographical Sketches of Men and Women Who Have by an Extraordinary Use of Their Opportunities Benefited Their Fellow Creatures* (London: Cassel, Petter & Galpin, 1860), 276; Oden, 128–129.

9   Porter, 269–271.

10 *Soulby's Ulverston Advertiser*, January 17, 1861.

11 Remond, 282; Ray Allen Billington, ed., *The Journal of Charlotte Forten: A Free Negro in the Slave Era*, (Dryden Press, 1953), 59.

12 William Wells Brown, an escaped slave from Kentucky, became an antislavery lecturer with a career both in the United States and in Britain. In 1852, based on his experiences abroad, he wrote a travelogue, *Three Years in Europe*. His novel *Clotel*, long considered the first Black American novel, was written the following year. C. Peter Ripley, ed., *The Black Abolitionist Papers* (University of North Carolina Press, 1991), vol. 4, 3–6.

13 Dorothy Sterling, *We Are Your Sisters: Black Women in the Nineteenth Century* (W. W. Norton, 1984), 281–288; Shirley J. Yee, *Black Women Abolitionists: A Study in Activism, 1828–1860*, (University of Tennessee, 1992), 87–89; Ripley, vol. 4, 38–41, 245. Also see Herbert Aptheker, *A Documentary History of the Negro People in the United States*, (Citadel Press, 1991), vol. 1, 161–163; Sterling, 116–119; Philip S. Foner and George E. Walker, eds., *Proceedings of the Black State Conventions: 1840–1865*, (Temple University Press, 1980), vol. II, 146.

14 Ripley, vol. I, 472; Foner, 208–209. Also see Fortin, 99; Brownlee, 94; Yee, 34–37.

15 Ripley, 40.
16 Louis Ruchames, ed., *The Letters of William Lloyd Garrison*, (Cambridge, 1971), vol. 2, 680.
17 Aptheker, vol. I, 197.
18 Billington, 103. Caroline Remond Putnum was Sarah's younger sister.
19 Dorothy Burnett Porter, "The Remonds of Salem Massachusetts: A Nineteenth Century Family Revisited," (American Antiquarian Society, 1985), vol. 95, 284; *Black Abolitionist Papers*, Microfilm, University of Michigan, 1981–83, Reel 10, for all of the following: "William C. Nell to Amy Post," Boston, September 22, 1857; "Report of the Proceedings of the Anti-Slavery Meeting at Rochester, N.Y.," February 10 and 11, 1857; and "Anti-Slavery Bugle," December 12, 1857.
20 Remond, 286; Ruchames, vol. 4, 600.
21 R. J. M. Blackett, *Building an Antislavery Wall: Black Americans in the Atlantic Abolitionist Movement, 1830–1860*, (Louisiana State University, 1983), 4; William L. Andrews, *Sisters of the Spirit: Thee Black Women's Autobiographies of the Nineteenth Century*, (Indiana University Press, 1986), 139–216.
22 For a listing of Black Americans abroad see Blackett, 209–216.
23 The organized fight for women's rights included the first feminist periodical in 1857 and a year later the Association for the Promotion of the Employment of Women. Clare Midgley, *Women Against Slavery: The British Campaigns, 1780–1870*, (1992), 170.
24 Ripley, vol. I, 5–6; Blackett, 209–216; Midgley, 125, 86–92, 142, 9–14.
25 Midgley, 99–101. For an excellent reading of the image see Jean Fagan Yellin, "The Abolitionist Emblem," *Women and Sisters: The Antislavery Feminist in American Culture*, (Yale University Press, 1989).
26 Clare Taylor, *British and American Abolitionist: An Episode in Transatlantic Understanding* (Edinburgh, 1974), 143.
27 Ripley, vol. I, 445–446, doc 74; 476, doc 81.
28 *Soulby's Ulverston Advertiser*, January 17, 1861.
29 *The Anti-Slavery Advocate*, London, November 1, 1859, no. 35, vol. 2; Ripley, vol. I, 435–440, doc. 73; 457 doc 77.
30 *Black Abolitionist Papers*, reel 11, "Warrington Times."

31 "Warrington Times," January 29, 1859; *Anti Slavery Advocate*, London, September 1, 1859; *Black Abolitionist Papers*, reel 11, "Miss Remond's First Lecture in Dublin."

32 Midgley, 163, 132–136. Bedford was the first college in England run by women for women. Remond boarded with Elizabeth J. Reid, abolitionist and founder of the college.

33 *Anti Slavery Advocate*, February 1860, 306; November 1860, 377.

34 *Black Abolitionist Papers*, reel 13, "Abolition of Slavery in America," *Non Conformisti*, June 19, 1861.

35 Sarah P. Remond, "The Negroes in the United States of America," *Journal of Negro History* XXVII (repr., 1942), 218.

36 *Anti Slavery Advocate*, February 1861, 399.

37 Sterling, 179.

38 Founded in 1863, the Ladies' London Emancipation Society had over two hundred members, the majority of whom had not been involved in the antislavery cause. Members and supporters included Italian nationalist, Signor Mazzini, and escaped slave, Ellen Craft. It published a dozen tracts within a year, and more than 12,000 copies were circulated. See Midgley, 180–183.

39 One government publication reporting on refugees in New Orleans documented 32,000 whites receiving assistance, 17,000 of whom had been born in Britain. The 10,000 Blacks consisted mainly of women and children. Remond, "The Negroes & Anglo-Africans as Freedmen and Soldiers Compiled by Sarah Parker Remond, Tract # 7 Published for the Ladies' London Emancipation Society By Emily Faithful," (London, 1864).

40 Blackett, 191.

41 Blackett, 191–193; Ripley, vol. I, 539, 540.

42 Douglass A. Lorimer, *Colour, Class and the Victorians: English Attitudes to the Negro in the Mid-nineteenth Century*, (Leicester University Press: Holmes & Meier, 1978), 181–182.

43 Blackett, 107. For African Americans who do point out anti-Black feelings see Blackett, 158–160.

44 Ripley, vol. I, 569.

45 Brownlee, 152.

46 *National Anti Slavery Standard*, November 3, 1866, Letters and Personals.

47 Roland Sarti, *Mazzini, A Life for the Religion of Politics* (Praeger, 1997) I, 102–105, 205.

48 *National Anti Slavery Standard*, November 3, 1866, "Letters."
49 *National Anti Slavery Standard*, November 3, 1866, "Personals."
50 Anne Whitney Papers, "Letter # 4: Correspondence Between Anne Whitney and Sarah Whitney," April 17, 1868; Dorothy Porter's research cites 1871 as the year that Remond "received a diploma certifying her for Professional Medical Practice" from Santa Maria Nuova Hospital. Porter, 288.
51 Lillie Buffum Chace Wyman and Arthur Crawford Wyman. *Elizabeth Buffum Chace, 1806–1899: Her Life and its Environment*, (Boston: W.B. Clarke Co, 1914), vol. 2, 42–43. Chace was the Rhode Island abolitionist who had, years earlier, arranged lectures for Sarah in New England.
52 Chace, vol. 2, 42–43; Villard Family Papers 6 MsAm 1321, folder 784, Francis J. Garrison to Fanny Garrison Villard, March 30, 1879 (Cambridge, Mass: Houghton Library, Harvard University). Edmonia Lewis was the daughter of an African American father and a Chippewa mother. For the meeting between Douglass, Remond and Lewis see William S. McFeely, *Frederick Douglass*, (New York: W. W. Norton, 1991), 310, 328–29.
53 Archivio Storico del Comune, Florence, Italy, as reported in Porter, 288.
54 The two sisters owned wig shops and manufactured hair tonics in Salem from the 1840s to 1885. Porter, 291–292.
55 McFeely, 329.

Chapter 3

1 Anna J. Cooper, *A Voice From The South by A Black Woman Of The South*, (1892; repr., New York: Negro Universities Press, 1969), 76.
2 For details on the impact of slavery on the daily lives of children, especially see Wilma King, *Stolen Childhood: Slave Youth in Nineteenth Century America*, (Bloomington, IN: Indiana University Press, 1995); Marie Jenkins Schwartz, *Born In Bondage: Growing Up Enslaved in the Antebellum South*, (Cambridge, MA: Harvard University Press, 2000).
3 Louise Daniel Hutchinson, *Anna J. Cooper: A Voice from the South*, published for Anacostia Neighborhood Museum Of The Smith-

sonian Institution (Washington D.C., Smithsonian Institution Press, 1981), 4.
4   See Mary Helen Washington, introduction to *Anna J. Cooper A Voice From The South*, (New York: Oxford University Press, 1988) xxxi.
5   The emotions felt by Hannah Stanley were also expressed by other slave women. Harriet Jacobs, another North Carolina slave, had a "shrinking dread" that knowledge of the "great sin" that led to the birth of her daughter would cost Jacobs her daughter's affection. Harriet Jacobs, *Incidents in the Life of a Slave Girl: Written by Herself*, ed. Nell Irvin Painter, (Penguin Books, 2000), 210–211. Long after freedom, Elizabeth Keckley chose to "spare the world" the name of the man who had impregnated her. She "did not wish to dwell on the subject … but if my poor boy ever suffered … on account of his birth, he could not blame his mother, for God knows that she did not wish to give him life." Elizabeth Keckley, *Behind the Scenes, or, Thirty Years a Slave, and Four Years in the White House*, (New York: Oxford University Press, 1988), 39.
6   Cooper, i–iii, 121.
7   Vivian M. May, *Anna Julia Cooper, Visionary Black Feminist: A Critical Introduction.* (New York: Routledge/Taylor and Frances, 2007), 88; Jacqueline M. Moore *Leading the Race: The Transformation of the Black Elite in the Nations Capital, 1880–1920*, (Charlottesville, VA: University Press of Virginia, 1999) 190.
8   Roberta Sue Alexander, *North Carolina Faces the Freedmen: Race Relations During Presidential Reconstruction, 1865–67*, (Durham, NC: Duke University Press, 1985) 77, 79–87, 152, 160–168; Anna Julia Cooper, "The Intellectual Progress of Colored Women," in *The Voice of Anna Julia Cooper: Including a Voice From the South and Other Important Essays, Papers, and Letters*, eds. Charles Lemert and Esme Bhan (Lanham, MD: Rowman & Littlefield, 1998): 203.
9   Cooper, 77.
10 Hutchinson, 30–34.
11 Ellen N. Lawson and Marlene Merrill, "The Antebellum 'Talented Thousandth': Black College Students at Oberlin Before the Civil War," *The Journal of Negro Education* 52, no. 2 (Spring, 1983): 146, 143.

Notes

12. Mary Church Terrell, *A Colored Woman In A White World*, (Amherst, New York: Humanity Books, 2005), 99.
13. Mifflin Wistar Gibbs, *Shadow & Light: An Autobiography*, (Lincoln, NE: University of Nebraska Press, 1995), vii–xviii; Ellen Henle and Marlene Merrill, "Antebellum Black Coeds at Oberlin College," *Oberlin Alumni Magazine*, January/Feb 1980, 18–21; For others who moved to Oberlin in order to pursue higher education for their children see Linda M. Perkins, "The Impact of the 'Cult of True Womanhood' on the Education of Black Women," *Journal of Social Issues* 39, no. 3 (1983): 20; Ellen N. Lawson and Marlene Merrill, "The Antebellum 'Talented Thousandth': Black College Students at Oberlin Before the Civil War, "*The Journal of Negro Education* 52, no. 2 (Spring, 1983), 146–148.
14. Hutchinson, 34–38.
15. Cooper also managed to outlive both of her peers. "Reunited Trio Blazed a Trail," *Washington Post*, April 4, 1952.
16. Also known as the M Street School and later renamed Dunbar High School, it was the only high school for Blacks in D.C., and the largest for African Americans in the nation. Among the faculty were Jessie Redmon Fauset, Ernest E. Just, Kelly Miller, Carter G. Woodson, and Mary Burrill.
17. Jacqueline M. Moore, *Leading The Race: The Transformation of the Black Elite in the Nation's Capital, 1800– 1920*, (Charlottesville, VA: University Press of Virginia, 1999). See esp. "Chapter 7".
18. As early as 1886, a year before going to live in Washington D.C., Cooper had begun to deliver public addresses and speeches. Lemert and Bhan, 345.
19. Lemert and Bhan, 310; Hutchinson, 108, 132; Not long after her arrival, Cooper's household included Lula and John Love. The two young people were the children of deceased friends in North Carolina. Leona C. Gabel, *From Slavery to the Sorbonne and Beyond: The Life & Writings of Anna J. Cooper*, (Smith College, 1982), 45, 67.
20. Anna Julia Cooper, *A Voice From the South*, Schomburg Library of Nineteenth Century Black Women Writers, (New York: Oxford University Press, 1988), 15.
21. "The Intellectual Progress of the Colored Women in the United States Since the Emancipation Proclamation," in Lemert and Bhan, 204–205.

22 Hutchinson, 103–104; May, 20–21.
23 Cooper, *Voice From The South*, (Oxford University Press, 1988), 101–102.
24 Ibid., 108–109; Mrs. N.F. Mossell, *The Work of the Afro-American Woman*. (Freeport, NY: Books For Libraries Press, 1971), 14.
25 Hutchinson, 131.
26 May, 23; Hutchinson, 111–115.
27 John Henry Clarke, *Black Titan: W.E.B. Du Bois*, (Boston, MA: Beacon Press, 1970), 192; "'Assailing London': The 1900 Pan African Conference" in Owen Charles Mathurin, *Henry Sylvester Williams and the Origins of the Pan-African Movement, 1869–1911*, (Greenwood Press, 1976), 60–85.
28 W.E.B. Du Bois, "The American Negro at Paris" *American Monthly Review of Reviews: An International Magazine* 22, no. 5 (Nov., 1900): 575–577; For the photographs displayed at the World's Fair see Eugene F. Provenzo, *W.E.B. Du Bois's Exhibit of American Negroes: African Americans at the Beginning of the Twentieth Century*, (Lanham, MD: Rowman & Littlefield, 2013); also Shawn Michelle Smith, *Photography on the Color Line: W.E.B. Du Bois, Race, and Visual Culture* (Durham, NC: Duke University Press, 2004).
29 In 1906, Du Bois made a trip to Europe that he described as sponsored "by grace of an English Friend." With the help of a bicycle, he "roamed throughout England, Edinburgh, the Isle of Skye and a bit of France." See W.E. Burghardt Du Bois, *Dusk of Dawn: An Essay Toward An Autobiography of a Race Concept*, (Schocken Books, 1971), 222–223.
30 Karen A. Johnson, *Uplifting The Women and The Race: The Educational Philosophies, and Social Activism of Anna Julia Cooper & Nannie Helen Burroughs*, (Garland Pub, 2000) 76–77.
31 Anna Cooper would have found educational facilities such as the "Monumental Industrial Institute In Memory Of The Old Black Mammy of the South" highly suspect. Chartered by a group of white businessmen and educators in Athens, Georgia in 1910, the intent was to pay tribute to "the old Black Mammy … who was valuable and worthy of the tender memory of the South." Funds were provided by sentimental Southerners distraught at the loss of "the Black Mammy [who] was trained in a

school that passed with the institutions of her day." Their goal was to train a new generation to *"receive her mantle."* June O. Patton, "Moonlight and Magnolias in Southern Education: The Black Mammy Memorial Institute," *The Journal of Negro History* 65, no. 2 (Spring, 1980) 149–155.

32 Anna Cooper's theories on Black education did not start or stop with Classical education. Both before and after the "M. Street" controversy, she explicitly supported education for the masses. Indeed, the Hannah Stanley Opportunity School founded by Cooper in the 1930s and named for her mother specifically invited those who were considered as slow learners. Leona Gabel, *From Slavery to the Sorbonne and Beyond: The Life and Writings of Anna J. Cooper, Smith College Studies in History* 49, (Northampton, MA: Dept. of History, Smith College, 1982), 77; Leimert & Bahn, 34; May, 68; Melinda Chateauvert, "The Third Step: Anna Julia Cooper and Black Education in the District of Columbia, 1910 – 1960" in *Black Women in United States History* 5, ed. Darlene Clark Hine (Brooklyn, NY: Carlson Pub, 1990) 261–276; Cooper, "What Are We Worth," 228–286.

33 Gabel, 47; In a book detailing his visit, Father Klein described being escorted by the Principal, "a negress, pretty, young and intelligent looking." He expressed surprise at seeing students moving between classes "in ranks, two by two, in absolute silence." Hutchinson, 58–59; For the observations of an English woman who visited the school in 1866 see Sophia Jex Blake, "A Coeducational College: Oberlin," in *A History of International and Comparative Education: Nineteenth-Century Documents*, ed. Stewart E. Fraser and William W. Brickman, (Glenview, IL: Scott, Foresman,1968), 337–346.

34 Johnson, 76–83; Hutchinson, 70–76.

35 Hutchinson, 83.

36 Gabel, 48–49.

37 Gabel, 67; Hutchinson, 108; Johnson, 67.

38 "The Third Step: Memoir of the Sorbonne Doctorate" in Lemert and Bhan, 322.

39 "What Are We Worth?" in Lemert and Bhan, 167–168.

40 "The Third Step" in Lemert and Bhan, 322; Cooper's starting salary was $750.00 a year when she began her career at M Street

School in 1887. While this was well above the wages of the majority of Black females in the country even with potential salary increases, stretching her funds to meet the needs of a suddenly enlarged family was a major accomplishment. Johnson, 69; Sharon Harley, "Beyond the Classroom: The Organizational Lives of Black Female Educators in the District of Columbia, 1890–1930," *Journal Negro Education* 51, no. 3 (1982): 256.

41. Hutchinson, 137–138, 187; Gabel, 44, 67.
42. "The Third Step" in Lemert and Bhan, 322.
43. Hutchinson, 140–141; Washington Post, April 12, 1925, "The diploma entitling Mrs. Cooper to her degree (would) be awarded by the District commissioner, to whom it would be forwarded by the University of Paris."
44. Lemert and Bhan, 327; May, 32.
45. In 1916, the school was renamed in honor of the African American poet Paul Lawrence Dunbar.
46. Hutchinson, 154–155.
47. Hutchinson, "The Frelinghuysen Years," 155–173; Melinda Chateauvert, "The Third Step: Anna Julia Cooper and Black Education in the District of Columbia, 1910–1960." in *Black Women In United States History* 5, ed. Darlene Clark Hine (Carlson Publishing, 1990), 264–273.
48. Chateauvert, 12.
49. Hutchinson, 173–175.

Chapter 4

1. In addition to graduating from Harvard University, Robert Herberton Terrell also earned a law degree at Howard University, taught law, and served as chief clerk in the office of the U.S. Department of the Treasury. In 1902, he became the first African American appointed to a judgeship in the nation's capital.
2. Debra Newman Ham, *Mary Church Terrell. A Colored Woman In A White World*, (New York: Humanity Books, 2005), 31–35; Annette E. Church and Roberta Church, *The Robert R. Churches of Memphis*, (Ann Arbor, Michigan: Edwards Bros, 1974), 3–6; Roberta Church and Ronald Walter, *Nineteenth Century Memphis Families of Color: 1850–1900*, (Memphis, Tennessee: Church-Walter, 1988), 16.

3   Ham, 40–41, 47.
4   Ham, 34–35, 31, 37.
5   Mary Church Terrell, "What Mothers Owe Their Daughters," *Unpublished Papers of Mary Church Terrell*, (Alexander, Virginia: Alexander Street Press, 2004), 78–80.
6   Ham, 37–39; Annette E. Church and Roberta Church, 14; M. Sammye Miller, "Last Will and Testament of Robert Reed Church, Senior (1839–1912)," repr. in *The Journal of Negro History* 65, no. 2 (Spring, 1980): 156–157.
7   Given his high visibility, such concerns were more than mere exaggeration. Robert Church not only supported efforts to bring aid and comfort to the larger and poorer Black community, but he was also capable of more direct action. On at least one occasion he joined two other Black men in challenging renegade policemen when they attempted to remove several Black women from a private gathering. Ham, 36; For rape and physical abuse of Black women during the riots see Hannah Rosen, "'Not That Sort of Women': Race, Gender, and Sexual Violence During the Memphis Riot of 1866," *Sex, Love, Race: Crossing Boundaries in North American History*, ed. Martha Hodes, (New York University Press, 1999), 267–293; Hannah Rosen, *Terror in the Heart of Freedom: Citizenship, Sexual Violence And The Meaning Of Race In The Post Emancipation South*, (University of North Carolina Press, 2009), see esp. Chapters 1 and 2.
8   U.S. Congress, House, *Report of the Select Committee on the Memphis Riots and Massacres*, 39th Cong., 1st sess., no. 101 (Washington D.C.: U.S. Government Printing Office, 1866), 1, 5, 35; Allen R. Coggins, *Tennessee Tragedies: Natural, Technological, and Societal*, (University of Tennessee Press, 2011), 214–218.
9   Ham, 68–70; Annette E. Church and Roberta Church, 12–26, 46–52; Roberta Church and Ronald Walter, 17.
10 Ham, 35–37, 39, 45, 56.
11 Cherisse Jones-Branch "Mary Church Terrell: Revisiting the Politics of Race, Class, and Gender," *Tennessee Women: Their Lives And Times*, eds. Sarah Wilkerson Freeman and Beverly Greene Bond, vol. 1, (University of Georgia Press, 2009), 71; Ham, 82.
12 Ham, 80; Founded in 1833, Oberlin was one of the few colleges to admit Black males and females as a matter of policy before

the Civil War. One hundred and forty Black women attended the college prior to the Civil War. Most female students, Black and white, enrolled in the Literary Course. Most often taken by, and referred to as, the "Ladies Course," the program was of shorter duration and provided graduates with a certificate. The traditional "Gentlemen's Course," required classes in classical languages and geometry and provided graduates with a Bachelor's Degree. Mary Church excelled in both Greek and Latin, but was less enamored with geometry. See Ellen Henie and Marlene Merrill, "Antebellum Black Coeds at Oberlin College," *Oberlin Alumni Magazine* (January/February, 1980); Ellen N. Lawson and Marlene Merrill "The Antebellum 'Talented Thousandth': Black College Students at Oberlin Before the Civil War," *Journal of Negro Education* 52, no. 2 (Spring, 1983): 142–155; Darlene Clark Hine, *Black Women in America: An Historical Encyclopedia*, (Carlson Publishing, 1993), vol. 1, 897–899.

13 Annette E. Church and Roberta Church, 32–34.
14 Sharon Harley, "Mary Church Terrell: Genteel Militant," *Black Leaders of the Nineteenth Century*, eds. Leon Litwack and August Meier, (University of Illinois Press, 1988) 307–319; Ham, 92.
15 Ham, 93–97; For an excellent overview of Black women educators in Washington D.C. during this period see Sharon Harley, "Beyond the Classroom: The Organizational Lives of Black Female Educators in the District of Columbia, 1890–1930," *Journal of Negro Education* 51, no. 3 (1982): 254–265.
16 Willard B. Gatewood, *Aristocrats of Color: The Black Elite, 1880–1920*, (Indiana University Press, 1990), 260–263; For a thorough description of the political and social infighting and larger economic conditions facing M Street School see Jacqueline M. Moore "Primary and Secondary Education," *Leading the Race: The Transformation of the Black Elite in the Nation's Capital, 1880–1920*, (University Press of Virginia, 1999), 86–111.
17 Ham, 99.
18 The school that Mollie Church enrolled in was founded by Empress Frederick, the British wife of German Emperor Frederick III. The recipient of a liberal education herself, the Empress established some of the first schools for the higher education of girls in Germany.

19 Later in life, Mary Church would record having received more than one marriage proposal while in Europe, only one of which she seems to have given serious attention. Ham, 101–102, 106, 110–111, 117, 119–128.

20 M. Sammy Miller, "Mary Church Terrell's Letters from Europe to her Father," *Negro History Bulletin* 39, no. 6 (Sept/Oct, 1976): 615–618; Ham, "In Europe With Mother and Brother," 115–124.

21 Ham, 138–140; Robert H. Terrell was born in 1857 in Virginia into a family of more than comfortable means. He began his education in Washington D.C. before attending Groton Academy in Massachusetts. Terrell was a graduate of both Harvard and Howard University.

22 Pamela Newkirk, *Letters from Black America: Intimate Portraits of the African American Experience*, (Beacon Press, 2009), 15–19.

23 Ham, 141, 143. In 1898, Terrell gave birth to her only surviving child, whom she named Phyllis after Phyllis Wheatley. A few years later, the family expanded to include the adoption of Mary Church Terrell's niece, also named Mary. Mary Church Terrell, "Lynching from a Negro's Point of View," *Quest For Equality: The Life And Writings Of Mary Eliza Church Terrell, 1863–1954*, ed. Beverly Washington Jones, (Brooklyn, New York: Carlson Publishing Inc., 1990), 167–181.

24 The *Indianapolis Freeman*, the first African American paper to incorporate illustrations, also included images depicting Blacks defending themselves. Illustrations reprinted in Amanda K. Frisken, "'A Song Without End': Anti-Lynching Imagery In the African American Press, 1889–1898," *The Journal of African American History* 97, no. 3 (Summer, 2012): 240–269; There is no one reliable source on the number of lynchings that took place at the turn of the century. Black journalist, newspaper owner and anti-lynching crusader Ida Wells Barnett compiled one of the earliest and most readily available records of the period. Using data kept by the Chicago Tribune Newspaper, she totaled 2,513 lynching between 1883 and 1899. With the opening year, 1883, showing the lowest number of 39 with an astonishing 241 mass public killings of Blacks recorded for 1892. See Ida Wells-Barnett. *On Lynching's: Southern Horrors, A Red Record, Mob Rule In New Orleans*, (1900; repr., Arno Press and The New York Times,

1969), esp. see "Lynching Record," 46–47; For statistics covering a longer time period see Amy Louise Wood, *Lynching and Spectacle: Witnessing Racial Violence in America, 1890–1940*, (University of North Carolina Press, 2009), 3.

25 Ham, 264.

26 The *North American Review* was the nation's first literary magazine. Originally based in New England in 1815, it subsequently moved to New York and circulated continuously until 1940. Issued intermittingly thereafter, the journal is still in print today. The *Review* was edited by and regularly received contributions from politicians, educators, writers and leading thinkers of the day. Those associated with the magazine included the likes of John Adams, Daniel Webster, Mark Twain and the president of Harvard University, James Russell Lowell; Mary Church Terrell "Lynching From a Negro's Point of View," originally published in the *North American Review* 178 (June, 1904): 853–868. Reprinted in Beverly Washington Jones, *Quest For Equality: The Life and Writings of Mary Eliza Church Terrell, 1863–1954*, (New York: Carlson Publishing, 1990), 167–181; Also see Martha Solomon Watson, "Mary Church Terrell vs. Thomas Nelson Page: Gender, Race, and Class in Anti-Lynching Rhetoric," *Rhetoric & Public Affairs* 12, no. 1 (2009): 65–90; and Elizabeth McHenry, "Toward a History of Access: The Case of Mary Church Terrell," *American Literary History* 19 (2007): 289.

27 Jones, 28; *Woman's Era Magazine*, March 24, 1894, November 1895, and November 1896. Originating in Boston, Massachusetts in 1894, *The Woman's Era* was the first monthly magazine published by Black women. Using the network of women's clubs, it was made available across the country; Dorothy Salem, "Community Action: Black Women Respond to Local Needs, 1890–1920," *To Better Our World: Black Women In Organized Reform, 1890–1920*, (New York: Carlson Publishing, 1990), 65–100.

28 As might be expected, the campaign to create a national organization was filled with strife as personalities and politics accompanied every phase of development. In the early stages, two separate organizations claimed to represent the national association before coming together as one body. See Salem, "National Movements and Issues: Women, Race, and the Nation-

al Association of Colored Women, 1890–1920," 29–53; Jones, "The Women's Club Movement," 17–29; Ham, "Club Work." Apparently, the struggle toward nationalizing Black women's groups did not dissuade, and may have inspired, the formation of similar organizations. Other national associations developed during the same time period include The National Association of Colored Graduate Nurses and Alpha Kappa Alpha Sorority in 1908 and Delta Sigma Theta Sorority in 1912. For Black nurses see Darlene Clark Hine, "'They Shall Mount Up with Wings as Eagles': Historical Images of Black Nurses 1890–1950," *Hine Sight: Black Women And The Re-Construction Of American History*, (Indiana University Press, 1994), 163–181.

[29] Jacqueline M. Moore, "Occupation and Enterprise," *Leading the Race: The Transformation of the Black Elite in the Nations Capital, 1880–1920*, (University Press of Virginia, 1999); Newkirk, 17; Ham, 224.

[30] Mary Church Terrell, "The International Congress of Women," *Quest For Equality*, (1904; repr., Brooklyn, New York: Carlson Publishing Inc., 1990), 189–196. Owned by two Black journalists and published between the years 1904–1907, *The Voice of The Negro* was a literary journal dedicated to the works of Black journalists, artists, activists and intellectuals. Contributors included Booker T. Washington, Georgia Douglass Johnson, Kelly Miller and W. E. B. Du Bois. Essays by Mary Church Terrell appeared in the journal at least 17 times during its four years of existence; Ham, 239–245.

[31] Mary Church Terrell, "The International Congress of Women: Recently Held in Berlin, Germany" *Voice of the Negro* (December, 1904): 454–461. Rpt. *Quest for Equality*, 194–195.

[32] Michelle Rief, "Thinking Locally, Acting Globally: The International Agenda Of African American Clubwomen, 1880–1940," *The Journal of African American History* 89, no. 3 (Aug. 1, 2004): 203–222; Ham, 371–372. Following W.W. I, the international suffrage movement redirected its attention toward the search for world peace. The Women's International League for Peace and Freedom was one of three major international women's peace organizations. Along with the other two, the International Congress of Women and the International Alliance of Women, the

WILPF, often shared membership and, on occasion, office space and publications. In fact, Terrell's 1904 address in Berlin was delivered before the International Congress of Women. Salem, 234–236.

[33] Ham, 374–375.

[34] Mary Murray Washington, the wife of Booker T. Washington, was a tireless worker for racial uplift and women's progress. Addie Hunton, a wife and mother, had traveled and studied in Europe in the early 1900s. In 1918, she was one of 3 Black women who went to France to support Black troops stationed abroad. She also worked with W. E. B. Du Bois in organizing the 1927 Pan African Conference held in New York City; For information on the International Council of Women of the Darker Races see Rief, 203–222; Cynthia Neverdon-Morton. "Advancement of the Race Through African American Women's Organizations in the South, 1895–1925," *African American Women and The Vote, 1837–1965.* ed. Ann D. Gordon, (Amherst: University of Massachusetts Press, 1997), 120–125.

[35] The conference that Mary Terrell refers to in her autobiography as the 1937 International Assembly of World Fellowship of Faiths may have been the World Congress of Faiths conference held in London in 1936. A dispute between world peace organizations resulted in both names being used interchangeably. See Marcus Braybrooke, *A Wider Vision: A History of the World Congress of Faiths, 1936–1996,* (Oxford, England: OneWorld Publications, 1997); Ham, 446.

[36] Ham, 451.

[37] The Ingram case was the result of a white farmer's attack on a Black female sharecropper. Four of her sons, ages 12, 14, 16 and 17, came to her defense killing the attacker. With no access to a lawyer and a one-day trial, the Ingrams were given the death sentence. Public outcry "reduced" the sentence to life in prison, but the struggle to gain their release continued. With the involvement of such disparate groups as the NAACP and the Communist Party, following a decade of struggle, Mrs. Ingram and her sons were finally released in 1959. Charles H. Martin, "Race, Gender, and Southern Justice: The Rosa Lee Ingram Case," *The Journal of Legal History* 29, no. 3 (1985): 251–268; Dayo

F. Gore "Reframing Civil Rights Activism during the Cold War: The Rosa Lee Ingram Case, 1948–1959," *Radicalism at the Crossroads: African American Women Activists in the Cold War*, (New York University Press, 2011).

[38] Jones, "What It Means to Be Colored in the Capital of the United States," 290; Ham, "The Colored Man's Paradise," 437; Michael Ezra, "Early Economic Civil Rights in Washington D.C.," *The Economic Civil Rights Movement: African Americans and the Struggle For Economic Power*, (New York: Routledge, 2013).

[39] Audrey Thomas McCluskey, "Setting the Standard: Mary Church Terrell's Last Campaign for Social Justice," *Black Scholar* 29, no. 2/3 (Summer, 1999): 47–56; Handed down by the Supreme Court on May 17, 1954, Brown v. Board of Education overruled state laws requiring racial segregation in public schools. The decision essentially declared so-called "separate but equal facilities" were, in and of themselves, not equal.

Index

A

Adams, John Quincy, legal counsel for Amistad defendants, 14
Alpha Kappa Alpha sorority, 61
American Anti-Slavery Society, 33, 35
Amistad Committee, 13, 14
Amistad, La, 7, 11, 13-16, 18, 20, 22, 23, 25, 26
  voyage of 1839, 8
Anthony, Susan B., 33, 66
Anthropological Society of London, 38
anti-Black feeling within the British population during American Civil War, 38
Antonio, cabin boy on *La Amistad*, 9, 10
Association for the Advancement of Science, 38
Ayers, Eliza, 19, 67, 80

B

Barnett, Ida B. Wells, 66
Beasley, Delilah, 88
Bibbins, Ruthella Mory, *Mammy 'Mongst the Wild Natives of Europe*, 2
Black snake. *See* Mar'Gru
Black Union Missionary Society sponsorship of Henry and Tamar Wilson, 18

Board of Education in Washington, D.C., 84
Broadway Tabernacle, 17
Brown v. Board of Education, 62, 93
Brown, John, 41
Brown, William, 24
Brown, William Wells, 31
Bruce, Blanch K., 51

C

Calloway, Thomas J., 55
Chace, Lucy, 42
Charles B. Church, Captain, 67
Chase, Elizabeth Buffum, 42
Chicago World's Fair site of Cooper's 1892 address to Congress of Representative Women, 52
Church, Louisa Ayers, 66, 67, 69, 73, 79
Church, Robert Reed, 66, 67, 69- 73, 75, 76, 79, 80, 84, 86
Cinque, 9, 16, 18, 19
  role as leader of *La Amistad* revolt, 7
City of Berlin, steamship, 76
Colored American, coverage of *Amistad* trial and aftermath, 17
Colored Women's League, 53, 83
Colored Women's League of Washington, D.C., 83
Columbia University, 58, 60
Committee for the Enforcement of

the District of Columbia Anti-Discrimination Laws, 93
Connecticut, legal status of Blacks in 1839, 11
Connecticut, life in 1839, 12, 16
Cook, Will Marion, 78
Coolidge, T. Jefferson, 80
Cooper, Anna Julia, 4, 45-73
   adoption of five orphaned relatives, 59
   as educator at M Street High School, 54
   childhood during Civil War, 45
   death at 106
   burial at Hargett Street Cemetery, 63
   disagreement with *Brown v. Board of Education* decision, 62
   graduate studies, 58
   hiring by Lincoln Institute after loss of position at M Street School, 58
   impact of emancipation, 47
   marriage to George Cooper, 48
   named president of Frelinghuysen University, 61
   paternity, 46
   Ph.D granted from Sorbonne, 61
   reinstatement at M Street School, 58
   status as outsider at Oberlin, 50
   study at Oberlin College, 49
Cooper, George A.C., 46, 48, 63
Craft, Ellen, 34
Craft, William, 38
Crawford, John, 38
Cuba, 8
Curaçao, 28, 43

D

D. C. school board, dispute with and firing of Anna Cooper, 57

Douglass, Frederick, 17, 22, 31, 34, 38, 39, 42, 43, 51
Du Bois, W. E. B., 54, 55, 57, 66
Dunbar High School, 61, 75
Dunbar, Paul Lawrence, 66

E

Eisenhower, President Dwight D., 93
Elaw, Zilpha, 5
Elaw, Zilphas, 34
Emancipator, The, 13
Exposition Universelle, address by Anna Cooper, 55

F

Female Moral Reform Society, Sarah Mar'Gru Kinson's membership at Oberlin, 21
First Colored Presbyterian Church, 17
Fort Sumter, 37
Freetown, Sierra Leone, site as repatriation zone of former slaves, 18, 23
Frelinghuysen University, 61

G

Gallaudet, Thomas, 14
Gardner, Nancy Prince, 5
Garibaldi, General, 40
Garner, Margaret, 36
Garrison, William Lloyd, 32, 37
Geneva Disarmament Conference, 88
Gentleman, The, 18
Gibbs, Ida A., 49
Gibbs, Josiah Willard, 14
Gibbs, Maria Alexander, role in education of Ida Gibbs, 50
Gibbs, Mifflin Wistar, presidential

appointment as U.S. Consul for Madagascar, 50
Green, Edward Henry, marriage to Sarah Mar'Gru Kinson, 25
Guilde Internationale, La, 58

H

Haliburton, Thomas, literary portrayal of Black female shipboard passengers, 2
Hannah Stanley Opportunity School, founding by Cooper, 47
Harvard University, 66
Haywood, Andrew, 46, 60
Haywood, Fabius J., 46
Haywood, George W, 46
Haywood, Hannah Stanley, 24, 46, 47, 62
Haywood, Rufus, 46
Hofstadter, Richard, 12
Howard University, 51, 61, 62, 75, 83, 85
Howard University School of Law, 85
Hunt, James, 38
Hunton, Addie, 88

I

Industrial Building and Savings Company, 51
Ingram, Rosa Lee, 91
International Assembly of the World Fellowship of Faiths, 89
International Congress of Women, 84, 85
International Council of Women of the Darker Races, 88

J

Jacobs, Harriet, 34
Jamaican uprising, 39

Jesus Maria, slave children as main cargo, 7
Jocelyn, Simeon, 13

K

Kagne, *Amistad* captive renamed Charlotte, 15
Kali/Kale, *Amistad* captive, 15
Kinson, Mar'Gru Sarah, 4, 7-26, 45, 49
   Connecticut imprisonment with other *La Amistad* captives, 11
   Education at Wheaton College, 19-22
   initial repatriation to Sierra Leone, 18
   marriage to Edward Henry Green, 25
   passage as kidnapped African child, 11
   public appearances as child reciting Bible verses in English, 17
   renaming as Sarah, 16
Klein, Abbé Felix, 1905 visit to M Street School, 57

L

League of Nations Association, California branch, 88
Leavitt, Joshua, 13
Lenox, Cornelius, grandfather of Sarah Remond, 29
Lewis, Edmonia, 42
Liturgical calendar of the Episcopal Church (USA), 63
London Daily News, 40
Lovejoy, Elijah, murder of, 12

M

M Street High School, 54, 56, 58, 60, 61, 75, 79

Mar'Gru, meaning of. *See* Black snake setting up new mission, 25
Massachusetts Anti-Slavery Society, 32
Mazzini, Giuseppe, 40
Memphis, 66, 69, 74, 75
  as haven for former slaves, 49
Memphis, 73
Memphis Massacre, 70
Mende Mission, 18, 19, 23
Minns, Chloe, as teacher of Black children in Salem, Massachusetts, 28
Montes, Pedro, 9
More, Hannah, 24
Moss, Tom, 80

N

National Anti-Slavery Standard, 41
National Association of Colored Women, 84
National Committee to Free the Ingram Family, 91
"Negro Anglo Africans as Freedmen and Soldier", 37
North American Review, 82

O

Oberlin College, 19, 20, 21, 23, 25, 49, 73
Oberlin High School, 73
Oriental, transport of Sarah Kinson on return trip to America, 19

P

Palazzo Maroni, 43
Pan-African Movement, 54
Patterson, Mary Jane, 49
Pinchback, P.B.S., 51

Pintor, Lazario, 43
Preparatory School for Colored Youth, 50
Prince, Mary, 34
Prudence Crandall School, violent public response to admission of Black student, 12
Puerto Príncipe, intended destination of *La Amistad*, 9

R

Raymond, Eliza, accompaniment of Sarah Kinson to America, 19
Remond, Caroline, 32, 43
  sister and activist ally of Sarah Remond, 33
Remond, Charles Lenox, 32, 33, 34, 43, 67
  abolitionist activities, 31
Remond, John, 30, 43
  Curaçao origins, 28
Remond, Maritche Juan, 43
Remond, Nancy Lenox, 5, 29
Remond, Sarah Parker, 4, 27-45
  appearances during first trip to UK, 35
  birth, 27
  death and burial, 43
  lawsuit regarding theater seating segregation, 32
  lectures in support of American antislavery press, 37
  letter published in *London Daily News* regarding Jamaican Uprising, 40
  marriage to Lazario Pintor, 42
  medical studies in Italy, 42
  membership in Ladies' London Emancipation Society, 37
  studies in UK at Bedford College for Women, 36

Remond, Sarah Parker of 1859 Liverpool trip, 34
return trip to U.S. for education, 19
Robson, William, 42

S

Salem Gazette, 29
Salem, Massachusetts, 27-31
  as Black Salem, 27
Selassie, Haile, 89
Sherman, Gen. W. T.
  1865 surrender to by army of North Carolina, 47
Smith, Amanda Berry, 5
Solvent Savings Bank and Trust Company, 71
Sorbonne, 4, 61
Spielberg, Stephen
  director of *Amistad*, 7
St. Augustine College, 63
St. Augustine Normal School, 48
Stanton, Lucy, roommate of Sarah Kinson at Oberlin College, 20
State Convention of Colored Citizens, 48

T

Taft, President William Howard, 85
Tappan, Arthur, work with brother Lewis, 13
Tappan, Lewis, 13, 14, 15, 20, 24
  work as abolitionist, 13, 15, 19, 22, 24, 25
Tehme/Teme, *Amistad* captive renamed Maria Brown, 15
Tent Sisters, 83
Terrell, Mary Church, 4, 49-93
  autobiography published, 69
  birth, 65
  death, 93
  education at Oberlin, 73
  effects of parents' conflicted relationship, 72
  elected president of the National Association of Colored Women, 84
  experience of racial discrimination in Germany, 78
  faculty position at M Street School, 76
  faculty position at Wilberforce College, 74
  impact on family of father's head injury, 70
  influence of grandmother, 67
  leadership role in defense of Rosa Lee Ingram and sons, 91
  lecture and writing fees as contributions to Terrell family income, 85
  loss of first child, 80
  marriage to Robert Terrell, 79
  maternal lineage, 67
  presentation of paper at International Congress of Women, 86
  privileged Memphis childhood, 69
  publication of essay Lynching From a Negro's Point of View, 82
  role within D. C.'s Black elite community, 82
  study in Europe, 76
Terrell, Phyllis, 85, 89
Terrell, Robert Herberton, 79, 80, 84, 85
textile industry, connection to slave-produced cotton, 37
The Liberator, 37
Truman, President Harry S., 91
Turner, Nat, slave insurrection, 12
Tuskegee Institute, 56, 60

V

Voice From The South By A Black Woman of the South, A, 46
  Anna Cooper's 1892 publication of, 52
Voice of the Negro, The, 86

W

Walters, Bishop Alexander, 54
War Between the States, Remond advocacy for the Union while in Europe, 37
Washington Negro Folklore Society, 53
Washington, Booker T., 57, 66, 88
  educational differences with Cooper, 56
Washington, D.C., 12, 50, 51, 53, 58, 61, 63, 69, 75, 76, 85, 92
Washington, Mary Murray, 88
Washington, USS, interception of *La Amistad* and towing to New London, Ct., 9
Wells, H. G., 66
Whitney, Anne, 42
Wilberforce University, faculty role of Anna Cooper, 50
Williams, Fannie Barrier, 52
Women's International League for Peace and Freedom, 88
Women's Mutual Improvement Club, 83
World Anti-Slavery Convention, 32
World War I, 88

Y

Young Men's Anti-Slavery Society, 37

Z

Zion African Methodist Church, 17

www.ingramcontent.com/pod-product-compliance
Lightning Source LLC
Chambersburg PA
CBHW071450160426
43195CB00013B/2073